Julien Gordon

Eat Not Thy Heart

Julien Gordon
Eat Not Thy Heart
ISBN/EAN: 9783744666145
Printed in Europe, USA, Canada, Australia, Japan
Cover: Foto ©Thomas Meinert / pixelio.de

More available books at **www.hansebooks.com**

Eat Not Thy Heart

by

Julien Gordon

HERBERT S. STONE & CO.
CHICAGO & NEW YORK
1897

COPYRIGHT, 1897, BY
HERBERT S. STONE & CO.

Eat Not Thy Heart

CHAPTER I

"I seen her in dreams."

"Well, if it don't beat all!"

"Only last week she was beckoning to me across the saxifrax patch down by the barn steps."

"Well!"

"My dreams, I tell you, ain't dreams. They're visions that comes in the night to betoken what will be." She had at moments a touch of that fervor in speech which had made of her father an orator.

"It does look quaint."

"If you take it, I'll slave for you." She got up and went over to the stove, where he stood in shirt-sleeves—not over-clean—and at whose dense, murky heat he was warming his rough fingers.

"The wages is high."

"Wages!"—a flash seemed to spend itself in the word.

"That's what they calls 'em."

"A foreman's a foreman."

"He says—gardener."

"What'll be *my* work?"

"The hens and other fowls, and the butter 'n cream. There's dairy women." There was a pause.

"Write and say you'll be farmer, and I'll kind of have an eye to the poultry-yards when I'm not busy . . . . write."

It seemed strange to Joe she should already make conditions; strange, but characteristic.

"If it's a gardener, I couldn't take the place. I ain't what's called a complicated gardener. I ain't used to greenhouses 'n flowers."

"I guess folks can do anything they've a mind to."

"Ha! ha! ha!"

"You laugh?"

"You're a queer one, Beth."

It was she who laughed now—an odd laugh, with an unpleasant note in it.

"You've said that all along."

"I guess I've felt it."

"It's your ma tells you I'm queer, but I ain't queer."

"I guess you're terrible ambitious."

"Well, your people won't die of their

ambitions—they'll be stuck where they're put."

"Ha! ha!"

"O, you *laugh!*"

He returned to the question of payment.

"It means wealth for the likes of us."

"It ain't wages, it's salary."

"I guess we won't quarrel over the name of it."

"What makes you afraid?"

He blew on one hand and scratched his head with the thumb-nail of the other. He cleared his throat and a quizzical glance shot out from his melancholy, sunken brown eye.

"You, I guess, Beth."

"That's silly, if I ain't."

"Things is n't what they look."

"There'll be the money and a home, a new house, the letter says, too, and I'm sick of this leaky place anyhow."

"We'll be their servants!"

"Joe, I believe you're trying to plague me."

"No, I ain't. A spade's a spade!"

"We won't then. The madam'll live close by. I guess some day she'll ask us in to tea. I guess we'll be real sociable with them. I guess they won't be proud with their own people. We will be all like one big family."

"Whew!" Joe whistled.

"You're set on plaguing me."

"I ain't, but I know them better'n you do. They won't touch us."

"How do you know they're so proud?"

"Hain't you read about them?"

"I've read about her on Sunday nights, in the Sunday papers, till my eyeballs ached."

"Well!"

"I guess she is lovely to look at, and .... good."

"It does beat me." Joe settled himself comfortably on a wooden-backed seat with his feet at the stove-lid. "You was always talking of her and the nice things those folks get, and now they've sent for us."

"Oh, my God!" she cried suddenly, with clasped hands, "Joe, Joe, take it!"

"All right." He puckered his mouth again, but this time emitted no sound.

She flew to him in ecstasy. "Husband," she excitedly cried, "kiss me."

He obeyed, kissing her cheek fraternally, but without ardor.

There was something in her that had always frightened him. Something that he could not understand, but which he vaguely felt should be kept in check. Joe was not analytical. This impression of danger was an instinct—no more—unreasoning as is that of self-preservation, the blind reaching of wild creatures toward high branches when an enemy is nigh. It has survived, the scientists tell us, in the upward struggle of the drowning. A mere memory of the monkey clutching at tree-tops.

Sometimes, in the close quarters of their poverty, when she forgot her modesty a little, and displayed her charms to him with more abandonment than he thought fit, at the hour of her morning toilet, or when disrobing, he would feel that in her lay something ill adapted to his poor cabin. It made him uncomfortable. His thin-chested, round-shouldered sister, his angular, battered, wrinkled mother seemed to suit more nearly the limitations of their sphere. Yet he was very proud of his wife—proud and fond of her—with, as I have said, an undercurrent of uneasiness.

Now, after this conjugal embrace, she went up to her bed-chamber, springing up the rickety steps as if borne on wings. On her way she looked in at a small bed which stood in her mother-in-law's sleeping-room. She neared it, stooped, and brushed a fly from her child's face. It was a fat, rosy face; the long lashes flecked with shadow lay along the cheeks which were puffed out like a cherub's blowing on a wind-instrument.

"She sleeps hard," she said, giving the sheet a pat and the blanket a pull, "she sleeps hard after her play."

In the morning when Mrs. Bush first awoke, got up, stretched herself, donned her simple gown, went with reluctant, lagging steps about her household work, her face was usually white. Her thick, black hair straggled in elfish wisps about her forehead. Her dark eyes were small and half shut, blind if the sun's rays fell athwart them. Her nose was uplifted and defiant, her lips pale and harsh. Her hands, in winter, were red with cold, dark at the knuckles; in the summer they were moister and more delicate. Her figure was always the same, impressive, almost stately, even when compressed into the ill-fitting cotton frock of the early hour.

After she had drank her coffee, however, eaten her breakfast of eggs and bacon, as the warmth of the day environed her, when digestion acted upon her nervous system, all this was changed. Her eyes widened and gained curious lights, unguessed before. Her nose seemed to grow chiseled and quivering, her lips red, while on her cheeks a damask rose hung out its brilliant hues. It was then that people said she was beautiful. Her mouth and chin remained her least alluring features. There was something unfinished about them. It was as if the hand of the cunning artist which had fashioned her had grown a trifle weary with his work just here, and had, with a few careless strokes, sketched rather than elaborated. The mouth was small but curveless, its line cold. The downward slope of the thin lips gave to the expression a certain severity. The chin ran with a somewhat angular sharpness to lose itself under the ear-lobes. It held a suggestion of defiance, of obstinacy, yet lacked firmness. But when her rich color came and went, when she was animated or pleased, she might still, in the imperfectness of language, have been called very handsome. There have been world-renowned beauties who have had far less positive claim.

"She is the homeliest and the handsomest girl ever I set my eyes on," said Madam Boyer laughingly to Joe Bush, when he announced to her his engagement. "I guess she ain't ord'nary, anyway."

"That she ain't," said Joe, grinning.

In birth, in education, Elizabeth was above him; that species of American education which troubles itself more with algebra than with grammar; and that birth which means some tradition of ancestry, a parentage not entirely illiterate. But in situation, if we can employ the word, she was not his equal. She was absolutely poor, and, beyond this, dependent; the orphan niece of people who had taken her in through charity, and who meant that their charity should bring its guerdon.

They were small farmers, eking out a living from the proceeds of a hundred acres which their narrow means prevented them from turning to its fullest account. Beth was her aunt's maid-of-all-work, slave, scapegoat. Still she was treated like an equal. She was their near relative. Equality was the motto of Pontifex society.

At the church sociables every one met on the same footing. The leading people of the village, Boyer, the lawyer, the minister, the Rev. Onesyphorous Legg; the postmaster, Mr. Hoge; the school-teacher, Mr. Frailey; the rival doctors, Bradford and Small, met the big and little farmers and their "ladies" upon the same plane.

It was at these, and walking to and from church of a Sunday, that Joe Bush's brief wooing had been accomplished. His mother was a widow. She lived with her son and daughter on a farm. Joe worked it. He also worked at carpentering, was something of a builder, almost an architect in the village where a flat roof and four walls were the sum of architectural development. When the old homes were despised for more modern tenements, Joe was generally in demand. But the pay was small. Sometimes the honor had to suffice.

Beth was not popular with the young men of the neighborhood. A certain superiority kept them aloof. There was a stiffness, a haughtiness which men resent. They said she was "offish" and "put on airs." They thought it foolish in one who was known to be miserable, overworked, and was generally shabby.

Her father, himself a farmer and at one time well-to-do, had dabbled in politics, which, in Pontifex, meant bad whiskey. A late repentance for this indulgence had turned him into a religious fanatic. He had preached in the market-place. His was a certain rude erudition, a gift of eloquence. He had died insane. Her mother was a Boyer. The Boyers were descended from French Huguenots, and had, as I have said, some traditions. Lawyer Boyer was a third cousin of Beth's dead mother. He spoke to his wife of the extreme suppleness, strength and shapeliness of his young kinswoman's limbs and bust; his wife, who was presumably not of French extraction, had never remarked them. It is safe to say that no one in Pontifex had done so. They would have told you that Beth was "a finely complected gal," and "had a sharp eye," which was intended for compliment. Her eyes were in fact only bright on occasions. They were often dormant and opaque, only discovering on rare occasions their hidden flame.

She hated her dependence at her aunt's. She still more heartily detested the aunt herself. Joe's offer of marriage meant release from thralldom. She accepted it without much coyness. His awkward homage had been on the whole pleasant to her. She looked upon him as upon an inferior creature, from which attitude was born a kind of protective affectionateness. Possibly she secretly realized that his was one of those unselfish souls, always at a disadvantage in the battle for existence; a poor investment. She pitied him. But pity, which is akin to love in gentle natures, in more impatient ones has a savor of contempt. Beth was impatient.

Now she went into her own room — hers and her husband's — and closed the door behind her. It was a forlorn enough place from the standpoint of luxury, yet it could not be said to be entirely tasteless. There was an attempt at decoration. It was not admirably ordered, but there were some cheap pink cotton curtains at the windows, some plants in a roughly-hewn box standing on the floor in the sunlight, a few fast-fading photographs, and brilliant, though frameless, chromos pinned upon the wall. On the double bed was a valence of coarse lace, a quilt made from variegated scraps of silk across its foot, the pillow-cases, or rather covers, had narrow tatting upon their edges. The valence and the quilt and the tatting were all Beth's work. She had nearly put her eyes out over them late at night when the babe was asleep and Joe snoring, and the housework done. She was not a nimble needle-woman, but these things she would have and . . . she made them. It was a necessity of her being to have something agreeable to look upon. According to her lights these accessories to her surroundings were agreeable.

This room was the only spot in the world where she could find solitude. Lonely walks are not the fashion among farmers' wives and daughters, and within their conventional rut of life would savor of eccentricity — then there was never the time — but here at snatched intervals Beth could be alone. Joe had early discovered that he was almost always in the way when he entered these sacred precints, and rarely ventured to do so before the hour of his evening toilet. That he should make some kind of a change for supper his wife exacted. During the noon hour if he needed to wash his hands, he did so at the yard pump. He could also throw off his boots and dry them in the warm kitchen. Here was Beth's only safe refuge from intrusion, and here she sometimes came to sit down and "think." There was at times a tumult in the young woman that needed stilling.

Privacy is the franchise of wealth. To the poor its liberties are unattainable. Let us hope that the generous laws of compensation which govern life give its equivalent! The rich so frequently cast off seclusion that it is possible its advantages are overvalued.

CHAPTER II

Now she moved quickly to a shelf which swung on two nails at the side of the bed, and took a book from among the others. There were five or six at the most, bound, but tattered and white at the edges. She sat down with this volume upon her knees. It was the Bible. She closed her eyes and opened it at random, putting her finger upon a text, unmindful of the page. She then raised her lids and read these words:

"And I looked and there was none to help me, and I wondered that there was none to uphold, therefore mine own arm brought salvation unto me."

Once more she closed the book, and opened it, her index upon the text; Proverbs, this time:

"Thanks to the Lord; for He hath shown me marvelous great kindness in a strong city, and when I made haste I said I am cast out of the sight of thine eyes. Nevertheless thou heardest the voice of my prayer, when I cried unto thee."

"Ah!" she said, and a smile played on her mouth. Mechanically she flecked the pages, turning now to the first blank leaf. It was covered with a small, irregular writing. The room was growing dark, the twilight was nigh. She rose and took the Bible to the window-pane. She remembered well the days in which she had written these words; how long ago they seemed! It was before her marriage, when she was still in vassalage:

"O God, help me!" they read, "I try to love and pray to Thee; some days I am all Thine, and I love Thee, then I get rebellious. Help me, O Lord, not to love beautiful things too much, not to crave them, not to envy others their fine houses and lands, and horses and dresses, not to long and long to have such for myself, not to want to be magnificent and grand. Make me humble. Kill my pride, or conquer it. . . ."

There was more in the same strain, somewhat hyperbolous, but well spelled, and expressed in far better English than she spoke. This anomaly is not uncommon among the graduates of our public schools.

Yes, how long ago! Already things were better, yes, better, shaping themselves. And, to-day,— to-day, hope had come.

Yes, she had raised herself by her marriage. She had a place now — was recognized. Her mother-in-law, who suffered the alliance rather than desired it, was just toward her, and, particularly since the baby's birth, treated her with more deference. For the elder Mrs. Bush was a just woman. Joe's wife was a daughter,—as such, a Bush, and, as a Bush, not to be gratuitously ignored or flouted. The Bushes were very plain folk — but proud.

Mary, too, Joe's sister, liked Beth well enough, and now that she was going to be married, looked to her sister-in-law for suggestions as to her outfit. It was conceded that Beth was good at "fixin' up things," and could "dress up pretty." A distinct tendency toward personal adornment lurked in her character. These manifestations of vanity were in themselves peculiar. She dressed for women, not for men, obscurely realizing that these value each other more for outward than for inward graces. Her mean apparel, while at her aunt's, had been to her a source of unending chagrin and humiliation. In her improved environment she enjoyed nothing more than the possibility of an occasional new dress. It must be said that the exigencies of Pontifex as to elegance were not great. The most advanced socialist could not have desired a more perfect system of levelage. Of course there were poorer and richer, but wealth was modest, conservative, old-fashioned. The few houses of importance were rarely thrown open. They had a furtive, apologetic aspect behind their shrubberies, all signs of life and animation being confined to their "backyards," as the small garden inclosures were called. Here Monsieur in shirt-sleeves sucked his pipe on the veranda steps, and Madame, in a sunbonnet, picked currants for Sunday's tea.

In this atmosphere Mrs. Joe Bush had been born, bred, and nurtured. Her early poverty had kept her more or less a prisoner. After her marriage, impending maternity, then its cares, the part allotted to her in the general household work, all had tended to chain her within the narrow limits of Pontifex parish. Strange as it may appear, the great metropolis, which was only a two-hours' journey, she had never visited but three times in her life. She had then passed the hurried hours in one or two of the large retail shops which offer to the purchaser every conceivable necessity. Heated and wearied she had eaten a hurried luncheon, after which, with the country woman's dread of missing her train, she had wasted nearly an hour, awaiting her husband in the ferry-house.

Once she had gone to the park and been driven around in one of the public carriages. She had been passably disappointed. She walked, with Joe shuffling by her side, a few blocks on Fifth Avenue. She looked up at the barred shutters and dusty hinges of the front windows and doors of some of its palaces. They seemed to her dreary enough. The absence of grounds about them, their neglected gloom, somewhat surprised her.

"I guess it's splendid inside," she said to Joe, who, with his hat pushed back from his forehead, was nursing a toothpick between his lips.

"Seems likely."

"I guess they give balls here."

"Mostly in the winter. The families is out at their summer homes now." It was August.

"How would you like to have that big one?" asked Mrs. Joe doubtfully, stopping in front of a white pile whose chaste serenity detached it somewhat from its surroundings. She thought it rather plain.

"Well, I guess I'd make a queer figure cutting pigeon-wings in one of them grand parlors."

"If what I've heard and read about those as occupies them is true, they ain't always better born or reared than you, Joe Bush."

"That's so; some men has a powerful grip to make money and spend it."

"You've never had a chance."

"I guess it ain't all chance. I guess it lies in the men," said Joe, with that sagacity which sometimes surprised his friends. For these friends, and even his wife, were wont to address him in the tone one uses toward children or invalids. Is it a tribute to innocence, or to weakness? It is possibly a form of respect.

"I guess all eyes is alike, but some has high walls in front of them."

"Well, I don't know."

"Well, I *do*."

"I guess I ain't one of 'em;" said Joe, following his idea; "you had ought to 've married one of 'em, so Dottie could have been a lady."

"She'll be a lady."

"Her mother's one, that's so," said Joe gallantly.

"And what 'd she and I do without you?" said Mrs. Bush after a pause, during which she had reflected that this last speech of Joe's deserved reward. He was not by nature an encomiast.

To tell others they are necessary to us unfortunately carries no conviction. They must be necessary to believe it. Joe, who was a modest man, shook his head protestingly.

"Pontifex is a bad place for them as wants to get up in the world," she continued.

"All places is bad," said Joe, with the profound pessimism of the tiller of arid soil.

"I guess these rich folks struck good ground at any rate," said Beth, smiling.

But Joe possessed one of those rare natures which draw no comfort for their own impotence by belittling the performance of others.

"I guess they knew how to turn it to account then," he answered shortly.

"What I said a while ago about walls is true, tho'," said Beth.

"I've seen 'em as had eyes that 'd pierce a stone fence."

Joe was right. Far-sightedness is character. Perception lies deeper than optical impression. His simple, reverent spirit often puzzled his wife. His religion—whose form was emphasized by eating strawberries and cream under bunting at church festivals to the sound of hymn tunes nasally intoned—taught him, above all, resignation; a patient acceptance of his lot; gratitude that it was no worse. If he looked upon going to church, as do most of the members of the Protestant sect to which he belonged, less as a certain duty and possible privilege than as a compliment to the "minister," its practice nevertheless bore fruits; sweeter, perhaps, and more precious to him than to those who seek transport in the grand chants and eloquent appeals of stately temples. Religion is life, not method.

Beth, although she consulted the Bible as a probably correct prophet of fortune—a practice that she and some of her schoolmates had kept up from childhood—was becoming, as time wore on, more and more of an unavowed skeptic. Church bored her, and during the Rev. Onesyphorous Leggs's long sermons she dreamed strange dreams for a poor farmer's wife. What we have not is what appeals to our imagination. It was with her lacks that young Mrs. Bush's fancy was paramountly busy. She was wide awake to the trend of the times. Her narrow existence longed for new interests, but these were material, and such as would pander to her vanity, which was more boundless even than her pride. Her point of view was purely personal, intensely rationalistic. She saw in the great movements which develop the resources of new nations and sway their fate only a means to private ends. Money seemed to her the only solution to the problem which fretted her, the only key to fit the door of that social advancement for which she secretly pined. As all lovers sigh for the wings of liberty which riches lend to love, so Beth sat restless on her hard pew bench, listening to the preacher's tirades against the powerful of this earth, who could with such difficulty get to heaven, as through a needle the camel, while on the other hand he prayed the humble to remain humble and bow to the hand of God. She admired the strong. "Nature's darling, the strongest," appealed to her clear sense, for as yet she had got into no direct conflict with him. She had hardly reached the door of the arena; the struggle and dust, the cries and rush that reign within, met her ears as a distant and invigorating tonic, giving her nerves throbs of expectancy. Now, during the one walk on Fifth Avenue, they were all on the alert, those high-strung American nerves.

"When I was in school, we read about the French Revolution. I guess it was just such people as these that got their heads cut off."

"Eh?" said Joe.

"They chopped off the king's and queen's, too."

"Is that so?" said Joe, interested.

"But I guess there ain't any cause for revolution in our free land."

"Everybody can be heard from here," said Joe.

"Well, I ain't so sure—"

"We've got a free press," said Joe, proud of this knowledge; "the working people is n't stifled."

"They'd better try it!"

But her cry was not of revolt. It was of hope. She as yet had no desire to destroy, only to build up—herself, her child—Joe would have to be dragged up. She faintly perceived this, but she felt herself capable of lifting weights.

Dismissing these topics of unimportance, Joe began to talk of a horse he had lately gotten in exchange for a cow.

"Farmer Green's folks is mighty mean. I can't say as he was high fed. If he war n't thin! He fell the first time I drove him over to the depot crossing, back of Smith's gate, but he fell easy and did n't do no damage. He only broke a strap, gagging. Since I nursed him up and fed him a bit I never seen a horse as could beat him, or do his chores. Now he's fat and slick as anything."

"That's good," said Beth, thinking of other things.

"I wonder," she said, as they swung and

staggered in the crowded car which was conveying them to their ferry, "I wonder if we passed Mrs. Archibald Marston's town house now?"

"What do you know about it?"

"There was a picture of it in Mrs. Boyer's *Herald* on Sunday. It's splendid!"

"You're always talking of 'em."

"She's real exciting to read about. I read of her wedding first, and I've kept reading till I know lots of things she does."

"I guess she don't do much. He's a capitalist. I suppose they have a mighty easy time, all play and no work."

"Well, no matter, I *like* her to have a good time."

"I can't see—" said Joe.

Here the car stopped with a creak and a jerk, and Mr. and Mrs. Bush made a run for their ferryboat.

CHAPTER III

It is not often that any of us attain exactly that meed of success which we have craved, or conjectured possible. Any gift, grace, or talent with which we start equipped can only be retained and made efficient through incessant self-sacrifice and vigilance. This assertion should doubtless be inscribed in that dictionary of "received ideas," which Flaubert, king of mockers, desired to dedicate to the inhabitants of Philistia. To those "imbeciles" who could thus—if ever tempted to the slightest originality—dip back at once into the tenebræ of platitude.

It is probable that Archibald Marston remained an unprovoked argument in contradiction of this assumption. He had made no sacrifices, had been only very moderately vigilant, yet all the good things of this life "had been added unto him." His programme, to be sure, early laid out, was mapped on large lines, and, curiously enough, it had not failed of its expectancy. For instance, he would have regretfully expressed the fear that he should lose his father at an early age. His father had deferred entering into nuptial ties until in middle life. When Archibald was twenty-three years old, his papa was duly gathered into the family vault where his father—the butcher—had rested for seventeen years. Is it necessary to state that this particular butcher had been a meat-dispenser of genius? He, too, like his grandson, had a large programme. A great general makes war, and does not rest content with the laurels of a single battle. This particular general had waged mighty wars upon rivals in the trade. He had beaten them all. A plain man always, when he died he left his millions to be divided between a son and daughter. To his portion the son added in wider enterprises of finance several more millions. He had expended a part of this fortune in the education and training of his son. He wished to make of him a fine gentleman. It may be said that Archibald had risen fairly well to this demand. He was certainly a man of presentable appearance and manner, with as much polish as the end of a century not distinguished for amenity permits. If he sometimes sat while women stood, lounged while they sat, did not always uncover his head when he bowed to them, and never saw a woman whose youth had waned, this was more a matter of pose than of politeness. He was not sure enough of himself to follow out the natural instincts of kindliness which lay in his nature, for if his was hardly a chivalrous character it was not a brutal one. And this pose—such as it was—good-humored at bottom, and not particularly harmful unless to himself, had served him well. He was essentially a favorite, and above all he was a man of fashion. He very rarely did anything clever, and never said anything wise; yet young girls liked him, young married women invited him, and his men associates called him a " good fellow." He could boast of no personal beauty. His figure lacked grace. He had a snub nose, his neck was too short and thick, his shoulders too high, and the calves of his legs were thin. He carried himself, however, with an ease that disarmed criticism. He was himself extremely critical of other people, an attitude usually impressive.

His plan of life was much less complicated than his father's or his grandfather's. It had, in fact, been made exceedingly simple for him. He decided early to go to college, to pass with as little study as possible, and to amuse himself to his utmost there and afterward. Having inherited his fortune precisely at the time it seemed fit to him to travel, he concluded to do so. He decided he would live in Europe for a few years—see life—the world—then return and settle in his own country. He concluded that the life of a country gentleman—for a large part of the year at least—would suit him best. He also decided that he would marry a handsome woman. There was one thing above all others that in this woman of his choice must be intact, and that was the escutcheon. She must be a lady. When he began to look about him, his eyes rested with favor almost immediately upon a young girl who had just crossed the threshold of womanhood. The second time he saw Lola Fenton he told himself that she was charming. A lady she certainly was. About her pedigree there could be no shadow of a doubt. She was on both sides of her house descended from a far nobler and more ancient ancestry than are four fifths of the members of the English House of Peers. Her direct American forefathers had been men distinguished in politics, diplomacy, and letters, and their women celebrated for beauty and elegance. They had also for several generations possessed sufficient wealth to meet the exactions of the world. She was the elder daughter of Mrs. Gardiner Fenton, a widow. From her mother she inherited personal loveliness, but it was not of the kind which strikes at first sight.

The most difficult subject to paint is that which requires demi-tints.

Lola Fenton's beauty was of extraordinary delicacy and refinement; pensive rather than brilliant, poetic rather than positive, there was in it an element at once mysterious and fugitive. She was tall and thin; her hands and feet, her throat, her waist, were long, and so were her limbs. Her head was small, crowned with fine soft hair in which there was little color. It was of an ashy, dead-leaf hue. Her forehead was low and broad, her eyes dreamy and gentle, of a violet gray outlined by bluish shadows. Her nose was small and tipped upward. Her mouth was exquisitely tender and somewhat sad. Wide in repose, when she spoke or smiled she drew the lips together and pouted them out as does a child who sues for a kiss. In the expression of her face there was something indefinably touching. Her complexion was pale.

In spite of her spirituality of appearance, Miss Fenton seemed to take very kindly to German cotillons, late balls, routs, dinners, dances, suppers, and the opera. She was everywhere an acknowledged belle. Before the end of her first season she was engaged to be married to Archibald Marston. Her mother's friends entered some protest. The butcher was disinterred. This was a cruelty to Marston, whose matrimonial venture was intended to conclusively sink this inconvenient predecessor.

"How was it possible," they asked, "that Lola should so drag her family into the dust?" It had to be conceded, however, that the dust, such as it was, was golden. The dust and its quality, however, had not been weighed in the young girl's balances. She was passionately in love. At this people marveled. The "What can she see in him?" gathered force with every reiteration until a torrent of questions rose and broke on the strand of social exigence.

This question, always enigmatic, was as difficult of solution as is the one which asks why one woman is a success in the world while another is distanced in the race. The mere answer that she possesses social talent does not seem to cover the ground. Miss Fenton herself was far less beautiful than many of her maiden rivals. She was not a wit. Never could it be said of any feminine creature that she made less effort. She seemed to be one of those exceptional beings who are born attractive, who have but to cross a threshold to be surrounded, raise her eyes to be adored. It was this very lack of aggressiveness which captured Marston. He was accustomed to other methods. Mothers and daughters had not been cold to him. For though they might now in the hour of their disaffection ask, "What can she see in him?" they had been fully aware of the solid advantages which he could offer them.

To be in love with her husband is not favorable to the career of a young matron. It is apt to make her watchful where blindness is incumbent, eager where zeal is out of place, and a sure subject of raillery to the heart-free. It is possible that Lola Fenton's bark, when she became Mrs. Archibald Marston, might have sunk in this quicksand had not her husband's guiding hand been at the helm. He saw to it that their devotion was not too pronounced in public. Her own reserve would hardly have countenanced exhibitions of affection, but what he desired was a clever and haughty mistress to his establishment, not a love-sick wife. He wanted a partner, not to sing madrigals.

In the first year of their marriage she did not quite understand. Her mind, though thoughtful, was not quick to meteoric impressions, and so she managed to be very happy with her husband, in spite of him. As contentment is the vital atmosphere of the soul, she bloomed like a lily in the dew. What physician is worth one drop of joy! Health cast its soft flush on her cheeks. Marriage opened up life for her. She grew in mind and heart, and was transfigured. To those who help such growth in us we should be grateful. Lola was grateful.

When he took her to the splendid home he built for her in the country, her cup seemed indeed brimful of pleasure. She loved nature. She loved the moonlit fields, the breath of flowers under wet leaves, the crisp odors of the sea at ebb-tide, and to her love for her lover were now added all these beautiful things. It was only the over-bubbling of this inward content which she gave to the world. Her husband supplied her deficiencies. It was he who superintended her list and scratched out and erased undesirable names. It was he who organized the house, ordered the dinners, and it was even he who superintended some of the subtle details of his wife's toilettes. She thanked him without many words, pouting out her lips and smiling at him from out of her deep eyes. He had known a few passions of straw, and they had blazed up and dried his heart—a little—but it was, as hearts go, fairly juicy still. Not imaginative, not given to overmuch emotion, he had, like many men, sought the stimulus of sensation. If his disillusions were less violent than those of men of imagination, they were at least sufficiently succinct to make him appreciate the companionship of his exquisite young wife. He was glad to settle down, for he was by nature fond of order. His tastes were respectable. He was honorable in money matters. He had the horror of debt and of confusion of the man who has always been sure of his meals and whose debts have always been paid for him.

Not being in active affairs—an agent had the supervision of his vast estates—he could give his wife not only the fidelity which he had sworn—he respected the oath—but, what is more unusual in America, a considerable portion of his time. And here, after the early months of nuptial gayeties, housewarmings and bridal dances, the first little cloud appeared on the conjugal horizon. Mrs. Marston, in apportioning the seasons, planned for an occasional solitude *à deux*. She quickly found that this was to be denied; for while her desire for society was spasmodic and intermittent, her husband's seemed to be permanent. He was always inviting guests, and when she had organized a dainty feast for two, three or four were sure to enjoy it, through Mr. Marston's interference. He seemed never tired of the evident admiration which she inspired; how then could she be ungracious? Between Lola and her husband there was fortunately none of that acute temperamental antagonism which is probably physical, and from which spring unjustifiable hatreds. So she would heave a little sigh and hope that the next time nobody would come. Of a romantic fancy, Lola shrank from garish light. She sometimes wanted shadow. She wanted a lover who should lie at her feet, read to her from the poets, now and then just brushing with his lips her hand. Her hopes had held all the loveliest imaginations of the things we dream. Trodden paths, which her husband adored, looked to her a trifle worn. She told herself that these *fantoches* of the mind must be brushed aside like cobwebs, since they were in the way. Her husband laughed, called her romantic, and kissed her with a light jest. She took the kiss, which warmed her heart—in spite of all it was growing a little chill—and told herself with a faint sigh that her dreams had been but the radiant aurora of all early youth. In a few years she had sacrificed her hopes, she had resigned herself to be forever before the footlights. The desire for a more intellectual comradeship became fainter as the weariness of the crowd's encroachments increased. It was certainly a very exclusive crowd, elegant and esthetically satisfactory, if not quite congenial. As is often the case, the inferior nature had vanquished. Marston remained master of the field. He certainly had taste. It was exemplified by the selections he made during their short trips across the Atlantic, of paintings, statuary, rare tapestries, porcelains, and furniture for their city and country homes. These were marvels. Lola did not cease to vaunt her husband's artistic perceptions. Sometimes indeed, when not otherwise engaged, Mr. Marston discoursed on art. He pooh-poohed the moderns. Paris! phew! a millinery shop! Rome! there was the school to which all art must turn; from the men who build and decorate to those who paint and chisel, from the men who mould soft potteries to those who chink hard metals. Without Italy's suggestions where would David have drawn the classic impulse with which he conquered France, or Asmus Carstens that which made him father of German art? He discoursed wisely on Rome's architecture; of the use of columns in front of closed walls, of the construction of domes above circular interiors, dwelt on cylindrical and groined vaultings. He spoke of early Christian influence, and of Byzantine outgrowths; of forensic basilica, of cancelli, of ambones. He dwelt on Bondone and Bramante, and sighed that the giants were all dead! He flagellated Correggio, called him "a modern," "unrefined," "lacking in repose." He patted Paolo Caliari on the back, approving of his spirit and his richness. He chattered of the Greeks; Polycletus, Myron, Alcamanes— "Give me the lofty," he would say, " I don't want the pretty." Then he would descant on the portrait busts in terra-cotta of the Gregorian collection, of the painted vases of Etruria; marveling at fools who did not know that those representing black figures on a red ground are of a greater antiquity than those which reverse these colors. When their host mounted this art horse, I regret to state that his audience was usually stifling yawns, while his wife, with eyes that begged approval, nodded, with faint smiles and dovelike cooings, her rapturous admiration. Wrapped in absorbed attention, "See," she would seem to say, "what a man I married!" The fact is that what Marston knew of art was of the crudest and most superficial.

His old nurse—a privileged person who now presided over the nursery—was of this opinion.

"Laws! he's brought in more chucks," she would say to Lola irreverently.

"Why, Nursey, this is the 'Flight into Egypt,'" Mrs. Marston had once said to her, exhibiting a pre-Raphaelesque portrayal of the sacred journey, "and you call that chucks?"

"Egypt! Well, it ain't a bit like it then," said Nursey, who was a traveled person. "I guess he got cheated, poor dear, and it ain't the first time neither, he's that guileless."

"Maybe they hadn't got there yet," said Lola, examining the picture anxiously.

As years went by, Lola noticed that her husband's artistic harangue was always the same, that he did not expand his learning or teach anything fresh to his hearers; but she continued to gurgle and nod and encourage. Perhaps eye, speech, gesture, adhere to custom longer and more tenaciously than the mind, and are more lenient to routine.

Of the contents of his establishments it must be said they resembled somewhat the collection of an art salesman. When he had brought all these things home he had little genius at their disposition. His houses were like great museums through which his wife walked with a slight sense of oppression. She did not feel entirely at home in them. There was so much!

Marston secretly regretted that his wife did not lend herself more absolutely to his views of existence, but consoled himself by the reflection that the slight languor that she brought to her duties of hostess was essentially "good form." It seemed to distance and detach her from other and more eager women. Unappreciated qualities sometimes please by their reflex action. He forgave her, therefore, and thought, upon the whole, he could not have done better. Forgave her that she had discarded the trained nurses into the antechamber, and had herself guarded their only son—born in the second year of wedlock—when he lay ill with scarlet fever, thus endangering her own health and beauty. Forgave her that she would not leave his own, her husband's bedside when he had broken his collar-bone in a fall from his horse. The little son, Archibald, Jr., had his mother's small ears, long fingers, slight ankles and wrists. In him the butcher seemed to be effectually eradicated, for which Marston was very thankful to his wife. The butcher, indeed, was more and more forgotten, or only very rarely brought to life in the columns of some insectivorous sheet, whose sting was hurriedly torn off and thrown into the grate lest "the servants" should get hold of it.

This was the married pair whom Mrs. Bush had followed in the records of social-activities with such unceasing interest. They were, in fact, conspicuous and greatly envied.

CHAPTER IV

"I am glad to get home to America," said Mrs. Ayrault, leaning back and surveying the table with a satisfied inspection; "how nicely dear Lola does things!" she added, *sotto voce*.

Hospitality is a perfume. That of the powerful a quintessence to those who are its beneficiaries. Vanity is caressed.

"They tell me it's Marston does it all, and that Madame only sits up here looking her best. I fancied you 'smart' women," said Mr. Isham, whom Arden Ayrault had addressed, "thought it the proper thing to decry your own country."

"Pshaw!" said his handsome neighbor.

"I'm sick of the Continent," said Mr. Isham, "the Latins fatigue me. They are too excessive. They are violent, yet without impulse. They do not harbor force in love or friendship. This explains their infidelities."

"I understand you," said Mrs. Ayrault. "Hearts are weak, or is it nerves? They cannot resist or meet this exhaustless demand."

"I will say for the French"—Mr. Isham helped himself to a pickle—"that family ties are strong with them."

"The natural ones, yes," said Mrs. Ayrault. "Where marriage is an affair of business and *le mari* an enemy to be deceived or cajoled, a girl's mother remains her best protector."

"Then we Anglo-Saxons have a sense of justice even in our gossip. I'm weary of the personal 'persiflage' of foreign high life which slays the character as if it were a gnat. I'm descended from Puritans and am conscientious."

"Well, the English are heavy enough," said Mrs. Ayrault, "and occasionally in earnest. Why don't you try them?"

Mr. Isham blew his nose very loudly and coughed. He was a victim to chronic bronchitis. At least so he told his friends.

"The trouble with our cousins is that they are too commercial. They always want to sell you something. When I stayed with Lady Stockton, Sir John had a litter of puppies he wished me to purchase. I explained to him how inconvenient it would be to carry puppies about in traveling. . . ."

Mrs. Ayrault laughed.

"Yes, I remember Brownlow, Muriel Hatch's husband, the Earl, you know, actually made me buy a saddle-horse which his sister wanted to get rid of, before I left Drogo Towers."

"I thought," said Mr. Isham, "you had larger powers of self-defense."

"When a British eye is fastened on an American ducat, who shall be safe?"

"I confess I like their phlegm," said Mr. Isham; "the result, no doubt, of the constant exercise of the muscular system. Garrulity is unusual in England, even in age. The nervous forces are otherwise expended."

"Does not the work of the brain in artistic pursuits such as yours use up the energies beneficially?" asked Arden.

"No," said Mr. Isham; "nothing but body movement cures nervousness, curbs the tongue, and sweetens the temper."

"But what satisfaction you must have!" exclaimed the lady, bending toward the great artist.

"The desire for fame is doubtless the unacknowledged hunger of all humanity after the eternal—the immortal—but it is only won through degrading processes."

"Degrading?"

"Why, yes, in a measure. To curry favor with the public has always in it a note of baseness. They buy, we produce; a mere trade after all. They criticise, we shudder, hide it as we will. The performer is always an inferior to his auditor. Genius is the fool's slave. The fool sits safe. He has paid his way. He sits in his box with his Philistine smirk on while the poor actor sweats and trembles."

"Dear me!" said Mrs. Marston, their fair hostess, "dear me! How wildly interesting you two people are. Hush, Tad! Don't talk nonsense to me any more, I wish to hear what's going on at my right."

"Can't I listen too?" lisped Tad Nailer, with his vacant eye turned toward the bald spot above Mr. Isham's brow.

The great artist often came down for a day or two to Marston Terrace. It was almost the only visit he ever paid. He had the reputation of being something of an ogre, inaccessible and *sauvage;* but he admired Mrs. Marston and the peculiarities of this *ménage* interested and amused him. He also thought their chef made an excellent bouillabaise.

"The tip end of her little white finger is worth a hundred big hulks like his," he thought; "yet he plays Sir Oracle, and she looks up—delicious! delicious!" and as a keen student of human physiognomies and human weaknesses Mr. Isham always returned to the entertainment with renewed gusto.

"How you must study faces," said Mrs. Marston to him, "to catch and fix as you do fleeting and ephemeral expression! If an ugly woman comes to you, do you ever refuse to paint her?"

"It is astonishing," said Mr. Isham, "how a word of commendation will efface ugliness. We are ugly because we are evil-minded, morose, or unhappy. Flatter her a little, and behold she is pretty?"

"When you did my portrait," said Arden Ayrault, "you certainly did not flatter me!"

"You are vain enough already!"

"I like that!"

"Of course you like it," said the Count de Beaumont, who was sitting at Mrs. Ayrault's other shoulder; "women wish to be thought vain."

"Are we all alike, then?"

"Everybody looks alike to the ordinary observer," said Mr. Isham; "that is why life is so much richer to clever people. It takes original minds to see originality. The panorama is indistinct to the triflers. That is why brilliant intellect recognizes worth in simple persons whom the imbeciles only despise and trample upon. I once heard a silly girl say to Mrs. Jack Gresham that she had just read a story whose heroine was such a fascinating woman! 'But they are only attractive like that in books,' said she, simpering, while the arch-syren she was addressing passed on."

"You ought to have married a woman like the fair Constance, Isham," said Mr. Marston, not without a point of malice, "and given us the spectacle of two meteors twirling together in a whirl of astral space."

"We artists cannot give ourselves such luxuries. Love *à la Constance* is expensive."

"Artists are proverbially fickle," said Mrs. Marston. "They don't like to say 'forever.'"

"It's sometimes easier to say 'forever' than 'to-morrow,'" said Mr. Isham, with his quaint humorous laugh, "particularly when one's bank account is low."

"So, Sir Lemuel, you lost your happiness for glory?"

"Too few people, my dear Marston, know happiness to be said to have lost it. At best they lose a hope or a habit. My wife would have made me content, and herself too, possibly, if she had never asked me, 'Do you still love me?' If a woman asked me that exasperating question I should be hateful enough to think 'Do I?'—a propensity which springs from my New England parentage."

"I think you would make just the nicest kind of a husband in spite of your analytical propensities," said Mrs. Marston. "I shall take you for my second. As Archibald is pretty healthy, I shall be fat and middle-aged, but I shall never doubt the affection I inspire."

"Modern women have suppressed middle age," said Mr. Atherton, a widower, a man of the world, always a favorite in drawing-rooms. "Show me a middle-aged woman to-day. There are none."

"You see them still in the provinces," said Mrs. Plunkett, drawing her eyes away for one brief moment from the enraptured observation of her beautiful daughter, opposite. "You see them still in the provinces." She spoke as if alluding to some extinct bird whose claw-prints an ancient boulder might inconveniently have kept.

"Mrs. Gresham is artificial," Count de Beaumont was saying.

"That is why I like her," said Mrs. Ayrault. "I hate simple people."

"O, eccentric people amuse the outsiders, but are never popular in their own family," said Mrs. Maury; "the conservative qualities are better for every day."

"Artists should eschew the happy marriage. If properly understood and at peace, talent rarely develops to its utmost. It needs a little wholesome damming to produce the torrent," said Mr. Atherton.

"And the unfinished is nothing," said Mr. Isham reflectively.

"I suppose," said Mrs. Ayrault, "there are worse things than an unhappy marriage." Her own had been unfortunate. She was separated from her husband. "But there are moments when one thinks not."

"From what are called ruined lives spring charm and power," said Mr. Isham. "We are all condemned to suffer and die. What matter an hour sooner or later?"

"Dear me, how dismal we are getting!" said Mrs. Marston.

"That is the trouble with discussing life seriously," said Mrs. Plunkett. "One always gets dismal. But tell us about physiognomy, figure, gesture, Mr. Isham. Can you read character through these?"

"There's a good deal in it. There are types, of course. A man with large lips is usually false. A woman with full lips, tender. The big-headed, short-legged people, so detestable from the artistic standpoint, sometimes rule the world."

"Have patriots any particular aspect?"

"They are often commonplace in appearance, because they are rarely idealists. They are men of action, never philosophers. These last, the humanitarians, waste time in dreams."

"What's that, Isham? Discussing socialism, eh?" Mr. Marston raised his voice.

"Nothing was further from my thought." With another dry cough. "Plague on this bronchitis of mine!"

"You have a cold?" asked Mrs. Plunkett.

"Chronic—thanks, no, no more wine." This to an elderly and distinguished lawyer who had several times pushed the Madeira across the tablecloth with the deprecatory self-conscious attitude of the senior American who takes his pleasures as if he would say, "Here we are, my boys—wine, women, and song! Let's be merry while we may! Monday isn't here yet!"

"I'm conservative," said Marston. "I'm down on all talk of progress, petticoats, anarchism and incendiarism, women's suffrage, and labor emancipation. As for the socialists, I'd hang them all—every damned cur of them!"

Mr. Isham coughed persistently for two minutes.

"Don't you think, Mr. Marston, when more avenues are open to women, they will renounce vice, men will have fewer expenses, marriages will be more frequent?" said Mrs. Maury, one of the guests.

"Would *les cigales* go to work?" said Atherton. "That's the question."

"All women are born angels," said young Tad Nailer, blushing a bright scarlet. "It's us men who make them wicked!"

Mr. Isham looked at the speaker over his spectacles from under bushy eyebrows, with a glance half contemptuous, half approving. He drew in his breath with a short, wheezy sound.

"That's a good boy!" said Mrs. Marston, patting Tad's hand.

"Don't you think, Marston," said Atherton, "that we are ignorant of the laws which underlie the processes of evolution, and that much as you and I may deprecate changes palpably to our disadvantage, nevertheless change is inevitable?" He looked around as he spoke, at the magnificence of the dining-room which the ancestral butcher had furnished.

"I don't know anything about that," said Marston, fuming; "er—my—ancestors . . . were—er . . . self-made . . . yes, self-made. I'm not ashamed to own it."

His wife raised her lovely eyes to the ceiling. Now she knew he was faultless.

She prayed God to forgive her for having once, yes, once, feared her beloved was just a wee wee bit of a snob, and for having agonized over it. No doubt at the time her liver must have been disordered. Such injustice could have but one explanation—the bilious one.

The Madeira was in Marston's veins, and in his wine he was an honest man. "Why should others rob me of the results of their industry and wisdom?" he said, glaring.

Mr. Isham again blew his nose.

"Our forefathers," said Atherton, "were robust men, with a sense of duty and responsibility. We who profit by their labors are watched sullenly, but need have no fears if we emulate these qualities."

"Not at all, not at all!" said Mr. Marston. "I don't agree with you. It is the best men they wish to destroy; not the mean ones who let their wealth roll up while the poor starve; but the lavish, who scatter, are benefactors, and are therefore conspicuous."

"Deny the socialists as you will," said Mr. Atherton, "there are men among them who think and feel intensely. For this I respect them."

"Mere rhapsodies!" said Marston.

"Don't you think," whispered Mrs. Marston to Mr. Isham, "that it's often the best part of people which makes them conservative? Archie is so good to the poor! You don't know all he does! Nobody knows!"

"You see, my dear Mrs. Marston, what the masses ask for now is not alms, but opportunity."

"And has n't everybody opportunity in our country?" asked the host, catching his guest's remark on the wing.

"No!" bawled Mr. Isham.

"There must be selection," said Mr. Atherton. "How are you going to clutch the strongest and keep him down?"

"In the development of Western civilization our altruistic feeling will soon teach us," answered Mr. Isham. "As a great writer has lately told us, the very citadel is leagued with its besiegers. Intellect and reason, which are other words for individualism—every man for himself—are always selfish, and must be controlled by the extraordinary ethical movement which is the outgrowth of all great religious teaching. All excluded people will be brought into a wholesome rivalry of life. Even the broken-winded will have room to breathe, only we must not be impatient. The process of creation, which is still going on, is slow."

"I am glad I have no convictions, and can

hold my peace. It is all so bewildering," sighed Mrs. Ayrault.

"So was the French Revolution to onlookers, Mrs. Ayrault; so was the emancipation of the slave to his owner. I must say," said Mr. Isham, "the nigger has cost us a great deal. It was a good turn which was done him when he was brought over from Africa. He improved immensely over here. One almost envies an autocracy when one sees how the Czar freed the serf with a stroke of the pen, while we shed and expended, in our republic, oceans of blood and bagsful of money."

"But you surely thought slavery quite dreadful?" said Mrs. Plunkett.

"Of course it's dreadful, madam. It's dreadful to come into life and find yourself at the foot of the ladder with all the best positions out of your reach and already filled. The laws of the universe, as we regard them with our limited vision, are not calculated to make us very comfortable."

"Refined epicureanism is always the accompaniment of thoughtless wealth and power," said Mr. Atherton, who himself had a decided distaste for what he called the "common people," "and makes us cruel."

"That is coming right, all the same," said Mr. Isham. "Our evolution, it seems, must be very gradual. A slow, organic growth with a life-history at its back. Units have always been sacrificed. The cruelty remains and has to be swallowed. Let the poor devils take what comfort they can from the patience the priests preach to them. The French, where they have discarded such teaching, have presented a sorry spectacle. O, I don't find fault with them in idea, a wonderful people; but this restraining force they need, or else it is not others they destroy, but themselves. Christianity knew what it was about when it preached the beyond. Slowly but surely the liberal views are encroaching, advancing, conquering—a mere question of time. Slaves are free. Men have grown sensitive to wrong. My friend, Marston, here, who talks of stringing up anarchists, would not hurt a fly."

Mrs. Marston smiled, radiant.

"I saw him spend a half-hour yesterday picking a splinter out of his shepherd's hand. He was very gentle with the lad. He is not half bad-hearted."

Marston laughed a little shamefacedly.

"In England day by day we see the advance of democracy, a democracy born of kindness on one side, as well as discontent on the other. The conservative's is a forlorn hope. They are practically but the puppets of blind destiny, which stays their hand when it sees fit. Soon the hours of labor will be shortened; higher education will be more generally attainable; capitalists will give the surplus of their means to enterprises which will benefit the workingman, and, Marston"—he leaned over the table and fixed his host with his piercing eyes—"the ladies will have the ballot, and rule us more effectually than they do to-day."

"Here's to the success of your millennium!" cried Mr. Atherton, raising his glass. "I wish I was convinced."

"You said religion had taught us so much. You are from Boston, are you not, Mr. Isham?" said Mrs. Plunkett. "I presume you are a Unitarian."

"Do I look like a Unitarian, madam?"

"Why, how do they look?" asked Mrs. Plunkett. "Have they any distinctive mark on them? I know so many nice Unitarians."

"They look complacent, madam, as behooves men who have robbed the Lord Jesus Christ of his divinity."

"O, dear me!" said Mrs. Plunkett, somewhat agitated, "perhaps you are a Presbyterian?"

"I shall certainly not quarrel with my Presbyterian friends," said Mr. Isham. "They live in such material smugness, and give such excellent dinners! They assure me that this result of luxury springs from their scrupulous observance of the Sabbath. What do you think about it, madam?"

Mrs. Plunkett found that Mr. Lemuel Isham, of whom she had heard so much, made her a little uneasy, as we feel in the society of those we secretly suspect of laughing at us; yet nothing could be more impenetrable than his face, which was at once grave and respectful.

"While Isham delivers himself of his theories," said Mr. Marston, "I vote we adjourn to the smoking-room. Here, François, bring us lights."

The men adjourned to the *tabagie*, the ladies to the library, where the three mastiffs and little Archie's collie were warming their noses before a wood fire.

"Bush, the new gardener, arrived this afternoon, and desires to see Monsieur," said François, the *maitre d'hotel*.

"Ah, the new farmer," his master corrected him. "Tell him to wait for me a moment on the porch. I'll be there in a minute. I wish to say a word to him."

A quarter of an hour later he found Bush awaiting him, hat in hand. Mrs. Marston also came out and joined her husband under the stars. She and Joe Bush looked at each other. That first glance made them allies.

"What good eyes he has," she said to her husband afterward.

"Did she say anything about me?" asked Mrs. Bush when Joe had walked back to the cottage. She was still dressed in her traveling-cloak, finishing her supper with that feeling of strangeness and lost leverage born of arrival in a new home.

"I guess she had comp'ny. I guess she was busy," said Joe evasively. "No, she only stayed out a half-minute."

"Is she such a beauty?"

"Well, no, now, I should n't say she was a beauty. She's got a sweet-lookin' face."

Beth rose with a vague sense of disappointment.

CHAPTER V

BETH, who had a natural aptitude at command, found that the first days of her installation flattered this pronounced inclination. It was not only agreeable to be the mistress of a cozy and comfortable retreat, vine-embowered, freshly painted, crisply cleanly, with its porch on which Dottie might play—she found a distinctively suave flavor in being addressed as "ma'am" by the three dairy girls. The farm-hands, who were to be given meals at the cottage, were even more obsequious. They doffed their hats when she came out to wring and hang a scrub-cloth on the line which stretched its wires under the locusts behind the house. They called her Madam Bush, and wiped their feet on her door-mat when they crossed the threshold, with exemplary considerateness. She had entered precincts where order and law reigned, where there were some traditions of inequality. Such had scarcely existed upon the soil from which she had sprung. Josh, their chore-boy at

Pontifex, was a second cousin of her husband's. He never wiped his feet. When his work was over he came into the kitchen and ate and talked with the family. Now she found that she was not expected to sit at meat with the laborers and milk-girls, and was only to oversee their repasts from the vantage-ground of landlady. The maids took turns in waiting upon the table, and washed up the dishes when all was done. They slept in an adjoining cottage, which a stout, red-cheeked Irishwoman presided over.

"The big house," whose classic outline she could barely define through the foliage which half concealed it, seemed, indeed, during these first days, more unreal than when she had conned descriptions of its majesty in the thumbed pages of her Sunday *Herald*. Its engraved representation, which she had pasted in her old scrapbook, looked more genial and approachable. Her chagrin that its mistress had not spoken of her, on the night of her arrival, was followed by a sharp pin-prick. She learned that Mrs. Marston and her guests had gone away at dawn.

Before she was definitely told from headquarters, and in detail, what were to be her special duties, she would have time to "settle" herself, that vague word which, to feminine minds, conveys so much. To be unpacked is not to be established, to be dressed is not to be ready. On the whole it was well.

"I declare, the home is so pretty it's a shame we ain't acquainted around here," she said to Joe.

"I guess after the first church sociable we'll get friendly with the neighbors."

"There ain't any other grand houses like Mr. Marston's, is there, here?"

"I'm told two mile off some rich New York men's got mansions. I guess they're friends of the master's."

Beth laughed and flushed. "Why do you say master like that, Joe Bush? You ain't the gardener, you're the foreman."

The flower-gardener, Mr. Ackerman, had shown them about the place a little, and confided the poultry to Mrs. Bush's care. Beth was no novice in such matters, and she assumed with a good will tasks which seemed easy enough when viewed in the light of her past.

She amused herself Saturday afternoon after her work was all done arranging her sitting-room. She cut out a yellow paper cover for the mantel-shelf. She hung some green shades to the windows. The chairs, which were in sad disarray, she set against the wall with the accuracy of a methodic eye. The table she drew exactly into the center of the room, measuring distances with praiseworthy fidelity. Upon it she placed a cheap lamp, a family Bible, and two red-bound books on the subject of temperance, which an enthusiast had once left with her as he tramped by on a hot summer's noonday. She viewed books as bric-a-brac. To these she added a photograph of the entire Bush family, taken in a group, framed in braided straw. Joe in the foreground, with Dottie, ten months old, on his knee, and a curiously exaggerated right hand resting on the child's fat shoulder; and her own handsome features, just visible behind her mother-in-law's large bonnet presenting a livid blot. Two old brass spittoons she burnished up, and ranged on each side of the hearth. Joe had potted some plants for her. She stood these in the window, at which she hung up the cage of Dottie's thrush, which bird Josh had reared expressly for his little relative, and which the child had carried all the way from her home with patient watchfulness. It chirped cheerfully in the sunshine, singing on its perch in gleeful carelessness, while Dottie thrust her fingers between the bars, screeching with delight when they got pecked for their pains.

It was summer—Long Island summer. Hot, long days followed hot, long days. The cows made holes in the turf of their burned pasturage to cool their burning flanks. Far, far away the sleepy Sound sent up now and then a murmur when a steamer disturbed its quietness, lashing its peaceful waters into wave-crests.

Deserted by its owners, who had gone with friends to camp in the mountains, the great villa looked like a Greek temple, where it slept upon its low hill. From its stately terraces the prospect was magnificent, but they were not near to the sea, and when the Marstons wanted a briny dip they drove to the shore, on which they owned a private bathing-house. To the west of the house lay the Italian garden. The French windows of Mrs. Marston's bedroom, which opened upon an upper balcony, looked out upon its walks. This balcony was in itself a charming place. There were seats about it, and statues, and dark orange trees in terra-cotta pots. Sometimes of a morning she would bloom out upon it, clad in one of her pale-rose peignoirs, like a flower suddenly blown at the touch of dawn. While her husband was building the house, she was reading Percier and Fontaine, and the result had been the pleasure-ground, unique in America, and seeming but another apartment of a domain consecrated to ease. She desired box-hedges, and dreamed of arbor vitæ, but, like all judicious Long Islanders, had compromised on privet. This was so dense, finely cut and cared for, it was found to answer every purpose. In the center of the parterres, to which one ascended at four angles by stone steps, rose a fairy pavilion, where tea was served on warm and windless afternoons. It was a rotunda supported by Doric columns. Its interior was lined with mirrors. It was of white stucco, and glistened in the sun. It contained a marble table and seats which Mr. Marston had found in Rome. To the south the garden was bounded by several acres of uncultivated woodland. At the foot of its main walk was a rosery, in the middle of which a fountain played; about the fountain bloomed azaleas, hydrangeas, and such flowering plants as the season furnished. The basin was sunk to reflect upon the breast of its clear water the surrounding growths. Here and there at the edge of a bosquet, or opening of an arbor, one caught the gleam of white statuary — a dancing nymph, an airy graceful faun, giving the scene a festive and gay air.

"My husband has so much taste," Lola

would murmur to her friends when she showed them this garden, planned by herself. Under her calm exterior lay ever this ardent and anxious affection, asking sympathy. Mr. Isham understood her secret desire that all should do her husband honor. It touched him.

The glass graperies and conservatories were quite in another direction, skirting the eastern limit of the grounds. Through these, and through the flower-garden, Mr. Ackerman piloted Mr. and Mrs. Bush one Sunday afternoon. The French chef, Pierre Rose, was sitting in the pavilion in his shirt-sleeves, smoking a cigarette and reading his *Courier.* As the Bushes approached he picked up his jacket, put it on, and, with a low bow, was duly presented by Mr. Ackerman.

"*Quelle belle enfant,*" placing his hand paternally on Dottie's yellow curls.

He was a handsome, well-dressed person of about thirty-five, with a sarcastic mouth, a great deal of curly blue-black hair, and a general air of one who has seen the world and found it well enough. He joined the party, throwing away his cigarette, and sauntered with them along the paths.

"Who is he, anyway?" asked Joe of Beth, with a puzzled air.

"Mr. Ackerman says it's the—cook." Beth smothered a giggle.

"Well, if I ain't blessed!"

She could hardly snub this august individual, who was so much more polished than Joe, and far better dressed than any of the men she had ever associated with; yet her distinct contempt for "servants," and fear of their possible familiarity, rose in her throat. She contented herself by dropping back with Dottie, and letting the gentlemen walk in advance. By and by they met some maids from the house, strolling and chattering, looking very smart in their livery of black cashmere, wide white collars and cuffs, tiny ribboned caps, and embroidered aprons.

"I'd hate to wear anything like that," thought Beth, to compensate herself for the disagreeable impression that their outfit was far more tasteful and suitable than her own.

They stopped as they passed, and one addressed a soft word to Dottie, but Mrs. Bush pushed the child on with only a dignified and distant nod.

"Well, if she ain't a proud one!" said Bridget Summers.

"Mrs. Daggett never put on any such airs," said Delia. Mrs. Daggett was the late farmer's wife. She had been of Irish birth.

"They're Americans," said Mary, the under-laundress. "Augustine says so."

"Well, and if she be, she need n't eat us. We ain't exactly dirt."

"If those servants think I'm going to associate with them," Mrs. Bush said later to her husband, "I'll know it." She tossed her head scowling.

"I guess they would n't expect it," said Joe. "Ain't the men and dairy-girls been respec'ful?"

Beth shook her head. She did not understand anything any more. A sudden abyss seemed to yawn under her feet.

"Seems as if I did n't know what was expected," she said under her breath.

"I guess it don't do any harm to be civil," said Joe tentatively. "It's all one."

"It's a fine place," he said by and by, looking at his wife uneasily. "We never seen anything like it before."

But his efforts at conjugal conversation were baffled by silence.

Things and people all have two aspects: those of our impatience or of our tolerance. Beth's tolerant moods seemed, since her arrival at Marston Terrace, to be sorely strained.

CHAPTER VI

The church sociable, which Joe's prophetic instinct whispered would soon throw down the barriers of formality between the newcomers and their neighbors, did not fail to take place. They were bidden to it two weeks after their arrival. Here Mr. and Mrs. Bush made some acquaintances. They were treated with marked consideration. Mrs. Bush, who improvised a somewhat elaborate toilette for the occasion out of a piece of black silk, the gift of her mother-in-law, and some embroidery ripped from a discarded winter costume, looked extremely handsome. A certain excitement, indispensable to the beauty of her highly nervous type, lent itself to this result. Among the feasters whom she closely inspected, while they in their turn "took in" her striking figure, two persons detached themselves to dwell afterward with persistence in her memory. The rest was a bright mass of comely maidens in starched muslin frocks, which looked somewhat outgrown, belted at their slim waists with garish ribbons, and whose hats were surmounted by a large variety of bows, feathers, and cheap flowers. Some of them wore showy watch-chains, brooches, and earrings. The matrons, in soberer attire, with sallow cheeks, frequently—when over thirty—displaying in their smile a double row of palpably false teeth, generally wore black bonnets over thin hair whisked from a part two fingers wide. The men, rugged-handed, spare, with shrewd, kindly eyes, generally wore black broadcloth; some few of the younger ones, the lighter rough suits of the day's mode stamped "ready-made."

Two persons, I say, detached themselves from the crowd. One was a young woman, whose name was given to Mrs. Bush by the doctor's wife while they partook of coffee together under the tent.

"That's Floribel Pullen," she said. "Have you seen her before? She's well known around here."

Something in the lady's tone of voice suggested to Mrs. Bush that this knowledge was not altogether without spice, and might even touch on the forbidden.

"I have n't become acquainted with the neighbors, even by sight, yet," said Mrs. Bush prudently.

"Well, she's a gay one!"

"She's real pretty."

"How old, now, would you take her to be?"

"Well, I guess twenty-four, perhaps."

"Twenty-four!" If she had not been too ladylike to whistle, the doctor's wife would have relieved herself in this primitive fashion. "If Floribel Pullen ever sees thirty-four again, she'll be mighty content."

"Well! she's young-looking."

"It's a wonder, too, with all she's gone through," and again the physician's spouse raised an eyebrow charged with meaning. "Here, Miss Pullen," she called out to the object of her comments.

Floribel lowered a white parasol, and closed her eyes half-way.

"Did you speak to me, Mrs. Opdycke?" she asked in a clear, ringing voice.

"Yes; I want to introduce you to Mrs. Bush—she's living over at Mr. Marston's. Mr. Bush's taken the farm."

"I'm sure I'm very glad to meet you, Mrs. Bush," and Miss Pullen, extending a neatly gloved hand, courteseyed.

Where she got those gloves, that parasol, those fresh, perfectly fitting gowns, had long been an unsolved riddle to the minds of Paradise. The Pullens were known to be poor. The only son and brother was a ne'er-do-weel, the mother foolish and shiftless, with no known sources of income, the father dead.

She had white hands that did little or no work, as one could see by their finger-tips; while her well-shod feet, quick to tread the mazes of the dance, swift to run in the ways of pleasure, were laggard to all unpleasant errands.

Now she came forward, with her vivid smile, those idle arms outstretched to greet the stranger. Her enemies, and she had not a few—although of this she seemed unaware—could not but admit that she had a "manner with her." This manner was now uppermost. If it concealed turpitude, it did its work well. It was always modest, seemly decorous, candid. Yes, here it went a trifle far. There was a childish inflection of voice, upraised lids filled with innocent and unslaked curiosity, asking to be taught, to sit at one's feet, to listen—mayhap to be chidden and shed a tear or two. This attitude, which may have been a birthright, had crystallized into the *parti pris*. It still sufficed for the simple. The subtle questioned its values.

While she chatted glibly with Mrs. Bush, exclamatory, surprised — she lived in a constant condition of infantile wonderment—absorbed, sympathetic, eyes, ears, and tongues were busy with her name.

Miss Pullen's earliest recorded love affair had been a tragedy. While she was still very young, an admirer of hers was drowned. She appeared immediately in widow's weeds, insisting that she was engaged to him. The hostile and spiteful saw in this only a fine piece of comedy. They had doubted his intentions. He was the son of Mr. Paradise, a prosperous farmer, after whom the hamlet was named, a rich man, whose girls learned French, and whose sons were sent to college, far above the Pullens in position. Her lamentations, however, had been loud if not prolonged. She had exacted much commiseration from her acquaintances. A bereavement which fails to crush does not therefore stifle in us a desire for pity. Somebody must suffer if a just balance is to be obtained, and the dead to have their dues. She had risen from this blow with a certain smell of mould and mystery clinging to her garments. She was eminently occupying.

"If there ain't Florrie Pullen makin' up to Marston's new people. She'd be in with the last strange face if it had the devil's horns growing above it," said Mrs.

Bryan, the innkeeper's wife. "I don't say but what Miss Bush looks to be a right smart lady," she added, repentingly, after a hasty survey of Beth's straight back and shoulders. "I hear they're good folks down in Pontifex."

"Mr. Oakes is sweet on her now," said the addressed person, with a glance toward Floribel, in which malevolence was veiled in a certain satisfaction. Twenty years older than a husband who was not entirely impervious to feminine charm, the stout postmistress, Madam Fesser, although of a proverbially indulgent temper, could nevertheless defend her own when attacked, as her collie dog could fight for a bone. She was well content that Floribel's foray should be directed into another camp.

"He'd better look out then for that black-browed beetle as comes up of a Sunday after Florrie. Her ma says he's her reg'lar comp'ny, a lawyer from the city. I guess it ain't Oakes as'll cut him out. He ain't got a cent to bless himself with, the poor lad, for all his pride an' learnin'. They do say, tho', that the city chap is mighty sick of his bargain—"

Other women's men are apt to present an aspect of fatigue to vigilant feminine critics. Mrs. Bryan lowered her voice, and the two old dames with heads in close contact, and vibrant bonnet-strings, continued their talk in muffled murmurs, shaken by occasional bursts of shrill laughter.

"Mr. Oakes, let me make you acquainted with Mrs. Bush: Mrs. Bush — Mr. Oakes."

Beth looked up. This was that other individuality, besides Floribel's, which, from the moment of her advent on the church campus, had invaded and held her thought. A tall, slender young man, with unreadable gray eyes — eyes which burned like two fitful fires, curls of thick light hair, growing low on a forehead broad and prominent, a straight, finely-chiseled nose, a square, strong jaw, with lips drawn into set sternness; a rare smile, totally devoid of merriment, nevertheless lighted up the face into evanescent spirituality, giving it at moments a strange beauty; slightly stooping shoulders, the chest narrow and hollowed, but withal a nervous and muscular flexibility of frame.

The reason that these two persons stood out from among the country-bred circle of which they appeared to form a part was that Floribel, for all her candor, looked like a woman of pleasure, and Mr. Oakes like a gentleman.

Yes, in spite of his worn trousers, his

threadbare black coat, his sunburned straw hat with its faded ribbon, there was about him that discernible " quality " which is born in a person, never acquired. Possibly some remote ancestor, who had wielded sword or pen, at any rate power, had infused into his veins that drop of ichor which lifted him from among his fellows. Yet Percival Oakes was only a village school-teacher—as yet. In the heart-devouring weariness of his lot, while he hearkened to the drowsy voices of the dirty urchins and frowzy lasses who sat under his tuition, these two words, "as yet," flamed in his soul. That soul was full of bitterness. Ill-clothed, ill-fed, a chronic sufferer from acute dyspepsia, his face was already lined with the marks of morbid introspection, impotent cynicism, and impatient scorn. He walked through the beautiful meadows, his head crouched between his shoulders, or hanging forward on his breast, wrapped in dark musings. If nature was hardly a spectacle to him, it was never a refuge. His was not the reverie of the Oriental, to whom action is fatal and futile, but an agitated dream devoid of tenderness. His eyes, rarely turned upward to the heaven of stars, burrowed earthward. This habit gave him a frowning aspect, which passably alarmed children, and made young girls afraid of him. He was not over-popular. He was considered to be an inefficient teacher. It was said of him that he was above his work. Being alone in the world, without friends or money, he had been unable to obtain any higher education than a common school one, but by this he had profited. An industrious, steady student, he carried off every prize. He was still a student, an inveterate reader, and he perused deep, strange books, whose very names would have filled the mouth and disconcerted the brains of Paradise. His opinions were known to be of the most radical, and although he attended " meeting," there were those who whispered that he was a free-thinker, that he went to church as a mere form, and not to give cause for scandal to his scholars. He spent his petty stipend almost entirely in books, hardly giving himself the necessaries of existence. He boarded on the outskirts of the hamlet with a forlorn widow as lonely as himself. He was only twenty-three years old.

There was but one person who could boast that she had ever made him laugh. This was Floribel Pullen. Sometimes of an evening he called at her mother's house, and once or twice at dusk they had been met walking together in the fields. This had been enough to set the gossips at work, but there was really—nothing. Floribel enjoyed his incendiary, disconnected talk, which waxed a bit wild in its theoretic denouncements, its vain dissatisfactions, and in which the ego of a repressed nature played so arrogant a part. It is not the kings and great ones of earth who suffer from *la maladie des grandeurs;* it is those whom fate has thwarted. Nature revenges her own cruelties. In lunatic asylums those who play they are emperors and gods are recruits from the rank and file of the ineffectual and unfortunate.

Floribel thought him clever—which he was—while the young man was grateful to her for her unflagging spirits, her perfect amiability; and, shall it be said, the fact that she was contemptuously spoken of by other women drew him to espouse her cause. Notwithstanding that Oakes looked upon all merry-making as frivolous, her sparkling gayety was pleasant to him.

Now, when he and Beth raised their eyes, two little evil spirits, which dwelt behind them, looked out and recognized each other. They nodded and winked at each other, these spirits of revolt, shyly and furtively. Only there was this difference: Beth, who was much older than Oakes, had not yet reached his landmark. She wanted to scale, to rise, to reach; he wished to pull down, to scatter, to destroy—yes, he had traveled thus far already.

"Marston's folks is away, ain't they?" asked Mrs. Fesser, bustling up to join Mrs. Bush and the schoolmaster while they were exchanging a few perfunctory words. "There's letters lying for them at the office."

"Yes," said Beth, "they've gone to the mountains."

"Well, Archibald Marston's a good man."

"Good! why good?" asked Oakes gloomily.

"Well, he's a kind neighbor," said Mrs. Fesser, "anyway."

"Kind!" The word shivered with new meaning.

"He ain't ever done us no harm as I know of," said Mrs. Fesser, not without asperity. "No one likes to be so 'picked up,'" she told her husband afterwards.

"It's those kind men who ruin the earth," said Oakes with a scowl.

"I ain't one as dislikes a man 'cause he's richer than others," said Mrs. Fesser. "I guess if we had his riches maybe we'd do as he does, and not so well either. He ain't mean. It ain't them as splurge and spend as them dynamiters ought to blow up, but them as is stingy, and locks up their money in the banks where it don't do noboby any good." So Marston's views found echo in Mrs. Fesser's words.

"My wife's about right," said Mr. Fesser, coming up. He had lately been forgiven an escapade, and was glad to deliver himself of this tribute to Mrs. Fesser's good judgment. "When Marston built here land rose considerable. It's brought luck. Why, Farmer Sammis, he got four thousand for a bit of land no bigger 'n our back yard that did n't raise nothing nor shellfish and fiddlers, 'cause of its havin' a strip o' shore."

"Perhaps Mrs. Bush can tell us," said the schoolmaster with an enigmatic smile, "why land, which is the heritage of the whole human race, should rise and fall in values according to the whim of the few?"

It is probable that Beth did not understand him, yet a secret sense of being distinguished by his thus addressing her brought a sudden flush to her forehead.

"It does seem as if it were wrong," she said, half inaudibly, in that low, nasal tone which was her habitual one.

"And wrong will be avenged," said Oakes with stifled heat.

"My wife's right. One of them anarchy, cranky fellers gave a lecture over to Queen's on Monday night. Me and Charlie Bryan stepped in. Well, if he didn't say marriage ought'r be done away with, and men and women live free like savage folk."

Mrs. Fesser threw up a hand in protest.

"Well, if I ever! If that don't prove they ought to be locked up, I don't know as what does!"

Fesser greeted these exclamations with a series of virtuous nods. He was very comfortable on his wife's salary.

"I'm sure Mr. Marston's a good man, and his wife's a very fine lady," said Floribel, turning the subject from dissolving marriage ties with her usual tact. "Ain't she beautiful,' Mrs. Bush?"

Beth did not like to acknowledge that she had never seen the mistress of Marston Terrace, whom she would not have liked to call her own.

"Yes, she's beautiful," she said evasively.

Percival Oakes paled. Of a romantic temperament, all his dreams of equality, all his hopes for the dismemberment of existing law, all his passionate longing for redress, broke into nothingness before the phantom which Floribel's words awoke. He detested Mr. Marston with that deadly detestation whose enmity is none the less measureless because it is unreasoning. He resented his patronizing "How are you, Oakes?" and movement of head and whip as he passed behind his rapid horses, peppering the schoolmaster, plodding on the roadside, with summer dust, or splashing him with autumn mud. He loathed the man's self-satisfaction, the fashion of his covert coat, the cut of his short brown beard. He loathed him, and he loathed his friends. There was one in particular, one who was always with *her*, Mrs. Marston, whom he would have liked to spike, and split, and roast, like the bull-calf that he was! Mrs. Marston! near *her!* Ah! there could be no desire for equality here. This woman, toy of fate though she was, tossed in the hands of such miscreants—words had lost their meaning to his stormy consciousness—she indeed was born to sovereignty. None would deny it to her! The haunting sweetness of her mouth when she once addressed him in the train, thanking him for a slight service—he had raised a window the bull-calf could not manage—revealed to him her being. He felt that he alone understood her. She whose love should be a free gift to the trembling adoration of a timid vassal! She to be the slave of custom — the dupe of destiny! He pitied her!

In the young man's thought there clustered mistily about her person a boundless reverence, such as the early Christians doubtless felt in their blind worship for the queen of heaven. The one gentle, wholesome influence that filled his breast was that of this lady. It rested him. No Bernard de Ventadour, no Gaisses Brulez or Quienes de Béthune ever gave mistress a more transcendent homage than did this poor fellow to the woman who had spoken to him once. Sometimes he divined rather than saw her, under her parasol, in the sunshine, pacing her terraces, or lingering in her gardens; sometimes she passed him swiftly at evening in her low phaeton, under the boughs, or he caught glimpse of her, followed by her groom, galloping on her black horse across the twilight. At the mere thought of her there blossomed in his breast a mystic flower, a new ideal of manly honor, a new belief in woman's purity.

CHAPTER VII

"Here, Mr. Asch—Fenno, hand me that string."

"I can't reach it."

"Do you mean to tell me you are too lazy to get up and walk to the table?"

"What in the world are you heating yourself so for? It's infernally warm out here."

"Hush! Here's some one crunching on the gravel; it must be the Plunketts; but no," a laugh. "It's only our new gardener's—farmer's wife. Here, catch!"

Mrs. Marston threw a small hammer, followed by a garden trowel, over the ballustrade, at the base of which she was kneeling. These agricultural implements landed very near the nose of a young gentleman taking his ease in a hammock. This hammock swung in the veranda, a retreat furnished like a room, with tables, lounges, chairs, books, cushions, and a general aspect of careless comfort. He himself presented a picture of perfect repose. If in Mr. Oakes's dark cogitations the cognomen of "bull-calf" seemed applicable, to the casual observer it must have appeared groundless and unmerited.

There are not many finer specimens of physical manhood cast in the capricious mould of nature. His figure, admirably proportioned, has the lightness and agility of the Greek wrestlers trained to Olympian conflicts. Iphitus himself would doubtless have selected him for the ten months' novitiate which fitted to suppleness and strength the aspirants to the green crown. His face is no less remarkable; it is chiseled as with the deft hand of a Myron modeling a Marsyas. The hair, a rich bright brown, is abundant, silken, and curly; the mouth, albeit without sensibility, is absolutely correct to the rules of sculptured proportion; the lips are red, the teeth gleam from between them a flash of snow. The eyes widely open, of a dark sapphire blue, are of such flawless brilliance that they resemble glass-bawbles more than the pristine stone itself; they are surrounded by dark eyelashes of unusual thickness.

"What a beastly bore!" Mr. Asch turned over his white flannel form in the hammock, and glanced between its meshes with a somnolent eye. "Have I got to go away?"

"Why, yes, certainly; I've never seen her before. I have to tell her things."

"What things? I won't listen. I'm asleep."

"Well, they are certainly not corrupting to your innocence," said Mrs. Marston, laughing.

Mrs. Bush pushed open the veranda gate and mounted the two steps which raised its flooring from the grass.

"How are you, Mrs. Bush?" Mrs. Marston nodded; extending her right hand.

So at last Beth stood before her idol! She saw a tumbled blue gingham frock, from below whose hem pointed two slender shoes slightly whitened at the toes by contact with dew and sand; disheveled, somewhat colorless hair under a battered sailor hat; a delicate little nose upon whose slender *retroussé* tip the sun had just dropped a freckle. The hand extended was incased in a soiled *suède* glove reaching the elbow, wrinkled at the wrist. It is probable that the pit still expects the queen of the drama to appear in regal bravery; that a crown, an ermine cloak, or at least a scepter remain to it the only sure insignia of royalty. The vulgar conception of a pedestal is stilts. Although Beth had assured her husband, while still in the wilds of Pontifex, that she anticipated relations of intimacy and of friendliness with their new employers, possibly these exaggerated hopes had already paled. Mrs. Archibald Marston had too long filled her ideal of elegance and of power for the first view of her not to clash violently with all her preconceived imaginations and to be a fresh disappointment. As she shook the lady's extended hand with three cold fingers and followed her stiffly into the boudoir, she wondered who the " man " might be glaring at them through the hammock netting, and not rising when they passed him. She felt almost dizzy with her disillusion and chagrin. Yet strangely enough she had not been ten minutes with the fair *châtelaine*, had not listened to the ripple of her soft talk, the vibrations of her high-bred laughter, before she realized the distance between them to be enormous, and abysmal. No negligence of apparel, no lack of startling claims to beauty, nay, the very lack of these, seemed but to widen the separation, to accentuate the fact —a fact made clear to Beth's sharp insight, notwithstanding its apparent incongruity. Beth had herself made careful preparation for the occasion. She had once more donned the black silk dress, with its embroidered collar and cuffs. She wore a pair of tight and extremely *glacé* gloves. She carried her purse, in lieu of a card-case, between her thumb and index as if prepared for a shopping bout down Broadway; on her head was her best Sunday bonnet. It was rather high and had a bunch of red poppies at its apex. Her lips, dry with agitation, were pursed into their visiting angle, while her whole person assumed an unbending rigidity. Her hostess, on the contrary, was perfectly at ease; one hand went to her hip and remained there; with the other she pushed her hat from her forehead, giving a tug to the front locks of her hair which she dragged down to meet the root of her little nose with an impatient exclamation.

"I've been gardening," she explained, pulling up her skirt and crossing one knee over the other. "My stockings seem to be coming down, too," she said, smiling, and gave a jerk to the article in question, revealing as she did so a silken garter with a diamond clasp to it.

Beth froze upon her chair.

"Well, how do you like it here?"

A sudden resolve shot through Beth's consciousness. She leaned back in her seat, crossed one foot over the other, since this was the requisite "pose," but did it conservatively, only displaying the two first buttons of her perfectly fitting boot.

"Well," she said, "I'm trying to get

used to it. Of course it ain't like Pontifex."

Her tone somewhat surprised Mrs. Marston.

"Ah! Pontifex? That's your old home, is it not?"

"Yes, my husband's property is there," said Mrs. Bush vaguely, "and it is such a fine place— We have the very best society."

Mrs. Marston suppressed a desire to titter.

"Have you met any of the neighbors here?" she ventured. "I hope you will feel at home."

"They ain't the sort of people I've been used to," said Beth haughtily.

"Ah!"

"I sha'n't care for Dottie to associate with any of the children around here. They're rough."

"There are some nice children here, I believe," said Mrs. Marston, more and more *intriguée*.

"I'm very particular," said Mrs. Bush.

"Have you been to the church?"

"Well, yes," said Beth; "it's small. I guess the best folks here is Episcopals."

"And how is the dear dairy getting on?" said Mrs. Marston lightly, changing the subject. "I'll come over to-morrow and see you all there. And the poultry? I hope you're setting some ducks' eggs, Mrs. Bush."

"I will do all I can to please you, Mrs. Marston," said Mrs. Bush, "while we stay."

"Are you so discontented you think of leaving us?" asked Mrs. Marston, a trifle coldly. "Everybody loves this place, and thinks it quite charming."

Beth was silent. A painful pause ensued. She was the first to break it.

"You're real comfortable here," she said, superciliously, looking through the superb portières which divided the boudoir from the cold white spaces of the ballroom beyond. "But ain't these hangings hot in the summer? I wouldn't care to have such about me."

Mrs. Marston was speechless.

There were a few more words about the butter and chickens, then Mrs. Marston arose and said somewhat dryly:

"I'm awfully sorry, but I'm expecting friends and really I must dress myself. I'm so untidy. Come again, some morning—that is the best time—and bring . . . er . . . your little girl—what is her name?"

Then as Mrs. Bush sprang from her chair with the impetus of a ball shot from a cannon's mouth, Lola Marston made another effort at conciliation.

"I do hope they carried out all my directions about the cottage—the painting and papering. I was away and could n't see to it. I hope you found it clean and nice."

"It's some cramped," drawled Beth. "I think Mr. Bush's going to ask Mr. Marston for a new kitchen, and I think if he'd put us up a piazza like this you have here it would be much more like what we've been used to in Pontifex."

She inwardly thanked Providence that Joseph was not within earshot.

"We have had great expense lately," said Mrs. Marston, now decidedly roused, "and I have much doubt—nay, I am quite sure Mr. Marston will do nothing of the kind. Good-afternoon."

"Good-afternoon," said Mrs. Bush, with a slight inclination of the head. She did not know if she was expected to shake hands again, and half extended her digits, tortured into their six-and-a-half glove; but Mrs. Marston did not see, or ignored, the gesture, and slipped past her with a nod of dismissal.

As Mrs. Bush emerged once more into the veranda, Fenno Asch, who still sprawled in the hammock, woke with a start, and gave her an exhaustive inspection. She tugged at the gate for a moment ineffectually, but he remained prone, offering no assistance, watching her discomfiture with a smileless stare. When she got herself once more upon the turf, she could almost hear her heart beat. In its humiliation and its anger, she thought that it would break.

Fenno Asch shook himself. He liked Marston Terrace very much. They let you alone, and then the cooking was first rate, as was also the Madeira. At the other houses where he visited he was sometimes expected to talk to a girl, or—what was not quite so deucedly unpleasant, but still inconvenient—to make love to the lady of the house. One never knew where that game would end. But there were no such levies made here on his good-nature. There was no nonsense about Mrs. Marston, and when there were girls they talked together until the fools who like "girling" came up at dusk. These were in fact few. American flirtation—that white fire wherein no wings were singed—only occupation of old-fashioned house-parties—exists no more. "Le flirt," so painfully and laboriously emulated by the Parisienne, is to-day but spasmodic and spectral. It is only very ancient maidens and superannuated beaux who still wave the fan and flourish the hat under the mosquito awnings of damp piazzas and sunlit lawns, or whisper together in the secret places of the stairs. "Le flirt" is dead. "Le sport" has killed the pretty pastime of a frolic god. Young men and maidens, restless benedicts, and dissatisfied matrons meet to measure muscle. They wrest from one another the prizes of Tennis, Golf, or Badminton; ply the oar, swim matches, jump fences, and chat of the merits of their "wheels." When this is done, they yawn in each other's faces and turn for solace to a cigarette. . . . and their own sex. Wooings are brief, hidden, and end abruptly in rupture or at the altar. They are conducted secretly, and the gentleman in particular is wondrously ashamed of himself! He is mortified at a weakness which is not a part of "training!" Even the girl's vanity, if not exempt from the desire, is innocent of the practice of dragging her lover about for her friends to see tied up in blue ribbons. A marked reserve has come between the sexes, bordering on indifference. The heart flutter, the fevered pulse, the exhilarated brain are now reserved for more important tests of skill than mutual fascination.

Asch rarely went into the city, so it was just as well his hostess should understand he did not propose to do any day's work at home. He was probably the most absolutely successful expression of entire selfishness that could be conceived. His selfishness had reached a sublimity which made it admirable. He never did anything for his friends whose houses he slept in, whose stables he commanded, whose yachts he steered to the havens of his own desire—no, not even to send a flower at New Year's to their wives, a toy at Christmas-time to their children. In the world he recognized no obligations, and would have seen the daughter of a favorite entertainer partnerless a whole evening with delightful serenity. Lavish toward himself, he was parsimonious toward all others, never under any provocation yielding to an impulse of generosity. Yet women of position and of fastidiousness coddled, petted, and continued to invite him with tremulous assiduity. This was the more remarkable in that men are usually divided by women into two categories, and liked and disliked accordingly: the man with whom a woman feels her femininity and the man with whom she does not. The former is desirable, the second is an incubus, a stop-gap at disappointed house-parties or at impromptu dinner-tables. These classes or types have their subdivisions; the former, for instance, comprises the man who is simply temperamentally attractive to women without effort of his own, through qualities which are more guessed at than understood, and again the man who brings his intelligence to bear upon his intercourse with women and whose intellect is directed to charm them. The first pleases, the second holds. The first attracts, the second captivates, and is incontestably the more dangerous of the two. Now, there is no man at this moment alive with whom a woman feels herself less a woman than with Fenno Asch. Wherein lies, then, the secret of his success? There are men who have dared to say that he is stupid, but it is a question if persons who can thus suck the best from others, and live the parasites of an indulgent community, are really dull-witted. Fenno Asch is certainly not intellectual; he is grossly ignorant on nearly all subjects of reputed importance; but stupid he cannot be. I am myself inclined to believe him extremely clever. Just now, when my story touches him, he was the subject of peculiar solicitude. His long-suffering mother, whom he had for years treated with a neglect and indifference unparalleled, whom he had insulted, ruined pecuniarily, and deserted, suddenly married again. Loud then were Asch's complaints and moanings—"his home" was broken up, destroyed. More than ever must his friends now rally to his rescue. He did not mention to them the fact that his stepfather had twice in one short twelve months paid his debts; such bagatelles were only dwelt upon by sordid and vulgar minds. The women shook their heads and wept over him. "Dear Fenno! poor Fenno! What a nasty, wicked woman she must be, for driving him from his rightful place at his dead father's table!" They caressed him with renewed ardor—such ardor, at least, as he would tolerate; he was not himself ardent.

Once Singleton Ackley had permitted himself to express doubt as to the young gentleman's valor on the occasion of the sinking of a yacht when he had swum ashore and allowed two women servants to drown before his eyes. But in an excited chorus the ladies present reminded him that he once kicked a man; how then could he be a poltroon? Yes, Mr. Isham remembered it. The victim had taken advice after a feeble strike-out from the shoulder with which some clubmen, pouncing upon and dragging him away, had speedily interfered. He was much smaller than Asch. This fact was not dwelt upon. He, the victim, had himself carried in a hansom down to the old artist's studio. Mr. Isham, although gruff, was a man of the world, and was next best as an adviser to the polished expert, Ackley, who was out of town. He received the youth with a grim glare through his gold-rimmed glasses. The occurrence was laid before him.

"What ought I to do?" asked the victim, with a fretful whine.

"Young man," said Mr. Isham, still glaring, "there is but one thing to do under the circumstances—kill him."

The victim started.

"Is not that rather extreme—eh?" he whimpered.

"I've given you advice. I've nothing more to say."

"But—er—"

"Kill him and go to the devil, both of you," said Mr. Isham, growing purple, "for the two chicken-livered puppies that you are!"

The victim had prudently disappeared down the stairs with a rapidity unusual to him, and had hidden himself away in his cab. There had been no blood shed.

"She's the handsomest woman ever I saw," said Mr. Marston, coming up across the lawn.

"How many more times in your life shall

I hear you use that formula, Mr. Marston?" asked May Plunkett, appearing at the ballroom's glass door. She had driven over with her brother to dine. "Who's the beauty now?"

"My farmer's wife. I've just seen her for the first time."

"How's that?"

"They came just as we left."

"And is she such a stunner?"

"Superb!"

Fenno looked up. "What! that thin-lipped Yankee woman who has been worrying Mrs. Marston here for an hour? And waked me up in the best part of my nap? Why, Marston, you must be getting in your dotage!"

"Mr. Isham ought to paint her," said May Plunkett. "When I went to him he said he had done with professional beauties, that he would paint no more of them. He wants to get close to nature. What a sweet, gruff old thing he is, to be sure!"

The Marstons had been at home only twenty-four hours. That very morning young Archie had cantered up on his mustang to the cottage, and in a dialogue with Dottie invited her mother to the call whose success seemed now so problematic.

The Chesterfieldian manner, the aristocratic grace of the ten-year-old son of the house of Marston as he delivered his message would have surprised the ruddy butcher, his great-grandfather, when behind his bloody apron he wielded his carving-knife, cutting up joints, sirloins, and hind-quarters for a hungry generation. It surprised Dottie, whose brown legs shrank up in alarm, tucking themselves under her short pink frock while she sucked her thumb vigorously, and eyed the boy with a measure of distrust.

CHAPTER VIII

A few days after the encounter of the garden, Monsieur Rose, taking his evening promenade, strolled up to the cottage, intending to have a chat with the new farmer and his handsome wife. He had sometimes offered a cigarette to the late Mr. Daggett, while Mrs. Daggett mixed for them a glass of excellent grog. There was affability in his eye, geniality on his urbane features. Beth, from an upper window, saw him approaching. Joe, in his shirt-sleeves, was sitting on the porch-step, smoking a short clay pipe. He heard a rush above his head as if it were the rustle of wings, then through the mosquito-bar of the front parlor casement a husky command to "come in at once and shut the door after him." Never regardless of this particular master's orders, Joe prepared to obey with leisurely scrupulousness. As he reached the narrow hallway he was seized with no very gentle hand and huddled head foremost into the open sitting-room. His wife then began a series of signals and wild girations which she found herself finally obliged to translate into language if they were to penetrate the hide of Joe's well-known obtuseness.

"It's that cook, the French fellow," she said in a tragic whisper.

"Well, now, is it?"

"Hush! didn't you see? He's most here. Now, Joe Bush, this is to settle things. Am I a servant here or not? Am I to associate with cooks, or am I not?"

Joe stared. Life was assuming labyrinthine intricacy. To his straight mind it was becoming a hopeless entanglement.

"Eh?" He was trying to gain time.

"Do you expect me to receive this . . . creature as my equal?"

"Well I never! I ain't invited him to call," said Joe deprecatingly.

"You didn't! More impudent he for coming then, and so you can tell him with my compliments."

Joe opened his mouth, and it remained open, his eye hurtling about as if seeking a way of escape.

"So there!" His wife gave him another shove and flew past him upstairs to her bedchamber. She closed and locked its door with a snap, as if she feared the entire race of French *chefs*, armed with no honorable intentions, were in hot pursuance at her heels. The long-nailed fingers of Monsieur Rose had already fallen on the knocker.

Rap, rap, rap.

Joe stood irresolute. A silence—

Rap, rap, rap.

He cautiously crept to the window and perred out.

"Ah! Monsieur Bush," said Monsieur Rose, "*comment ça va?* Are you and Madame at home?"

Pearls of anguish beaded on Joe's forehead. He liked his place, the poor fellow! It seemed a paradise to him. He desired to be on pleasant terms with everybody, and his instincts warned him of the dangers of this internecine warfare. A snort from his wife's room, however, rallied his wavering spirit.

"Wait a moment, Mr. Pierre," he said through a chink of the shutter, "I'll be out." He stopped and put on his coat.

Monsieur Rose himself was faultlessly dressed. Joe greeted his visitor, but did not offer him a chair.

"Is Madame at home?" repeated Rose gallantly. "Am I disturbing an after-supper tête-à-tête? *Hein?* I thought I heard Madame Bush speaking. Surely I would not drive her away!"

Joe lowered his tones to a muffled key. "To tell you the truth, Mr. Pierre, my wife is at home, but she ain't visible."

"It will be for another time," said Pierre lightly.

But Joe felt that these futile if natural hopes had better be instantly slain. He could not bear a repetition of this ordeal.

"Well," he said, "I guess not."

Monsieur Rose stared, now more than puzzled.

"You see," said Joe, confidentially, "my wife's peculiar. She ain't used to the ways here. She ain't used to bein' friends"—the words stuck in his throat and choked him; all his inherent hospitality rose within him in an agony of protest—"to bein' friends with those as is in service."

Pierre was beginning to understand.

"You mean to tell me, Monsieur Bush," he said, "that your wife sends me this message—that I am dismissed? Do you know, Monsieur Bush, that she is *diablement* impertinent, is your wife, Monsieur Bush?"

Joe's head oscillated from side to side with a rotary motion, like some planet set loose from its orbit.

Pierre drew himself up with a jerk, bringing his heels together with a click.

"Now," said Joe, blandly conciliatory, "I

think she's wrong. I myself ain't got any such notions. I'm for bein' sociable with everybody, high or low, rich or poor. I'll always be glad to see you, Mr. Pierre."

For a moment Pierre had meant to strike him. Now as he met the man's sad regard, a sudden comprehension of his predicament, an odd emotion bordering upon compassion forced his hand back into his pocket, and, without another word and only a low whistle, he turned on his heel.

The splendid courage and the base cowardice of Joe's performance pierced his keen Gallic intelligence, filling him with a species of admiration and pity.

"*Sacre tonnerre*," he muttered to himself. "*En voila un qui a trouvé une mégère.*"

When Beth returned from her first visit to the big house, three weeks later, it is probable she had forgotten this episode. But Joe had not. When he remembered it the cold perspiration gathered under his round shoulder-blades.

The day after her call upon Mrs. Marston she asked her husband to have her conveyed to the station, as she desired to go into the city to make some purchases. She would take Dottie with her, and begged her husband to give her twenty-five dollars. He gave the money with his usual unquestioning docility.

She returned in the evening with a blue gingham, exactly the same shade as Mrs. Marston's, a pair of long, loose, tan suéde gloves, a parasol trimmed with lace, a pink paper lamp-shade with a rose on it, a glass vase for flowers, a locket for Dottie, and a sailor hat for herself. Dottie was carrying an enormous bundle. It proved, when unpacked, to be a mandolin, tied with a wide bow of mauve satin ribbon. She explained to Joe's astonished query that Mr. Oakes was a fine performer on this instrument, and had offered to give her lessons.

During those brief moments passed in Mrs. Marston's drawing-rooms, no detail of their luxury had escaped Beth's searching eye. She had returned to her abode with a sense of discouragement and of dismay. Her aggressive conduct—poor Beth did not know that in the great world no one is aggressive unless under penalty of instant expulsion—had seemed to make her at least partially victress in an encounter she felt to have been a duel. She now set about altering the arrangements of her domain. She pulled the chairs out from the wall, and set them here and there, awry—an incommodious method for the lumbering Joseph, who fell over them and bumped himself twenty times a day. She put the pink shade on her brass lamp, and filled the flower-vase with roses. She opened the slat of one shutter, and allowed a ray of light to enter. If it faded the carpet "it could not be helped," she told herself with desperate recklessness. She confiscated the family Bible and put two old magazines in its place, while the mandolin, with its satin embellishment, was displayed in the most prominent corner of the apartment. She had seen such a one in Mrs. Marston's boudoir. These things done, she set about making unto herself the gingham frock almost as exactly like Mrs. Marston's as she could well remember. The sailor hat was distinctly unbecoming to her severe cast of physiognomy. Nevertheless, she perched it upon the top of her thick hair, which, from being neatly brushed back, she now pulled and crimped into a loose lock falling almost to meet her large, shapely nose. This change of coiffure and the hat gave her face a hardness, a boldness, which Joe had never seen there. He sighed, but he said nothing. She had spent all the money he had given her.

If Monsieur Rose was not admitted, Mr. Oakes, on the contrary, was welcomed with almost overwhelming cordiality. He and

Floribel Pullen were invited to tea at six o'clock one evening, over which meal Mrs. Bush presided in her new blue costume, with Dottie at her elbow in a clean starched pinafore with yellow ribbons at her shoulders and the locket depending from her little brown throat. Mr. Oakes repeated his visit, and was again invited to tea. Even socialistic young schoolmasters, afflicted with a chronic form of dyspepsia, like cleanly and well-set tables, and it must be said that, while Beth was rather an indifferent cook of meats and vegetables, her pastry, biscuits, and preserves were of the best. Mr. Oakes, at any rate, added materially to his dyspepsia in their consumption, pressing Dottie closely in the race. Beth had meant to say a word to her husband of her first visit to Mrs. Marston, surcharged as it had been to her in emotional experiences; but when at the first syllable she met his dull stolidity, it was borne in upon her that there was nothing to relate—nothing to tell. Her own consciousness became as blank as his. Explanation seemed impossible. One person, however, she found able to gauge these subtler springs of feeling. Tentatively, almost timidly, she ventured to speak of them; of her pride, her sense of, and desire for, equality with the best, her ambitions for her child. She found herself instantly comprehended. No circumlocution was necessary. Mr. Oakes understood. To a woman this is precious. To prepare for hours, mayhap days, a phrase, a word intended to electrify a particular pair of male ears and have it accorded scant attention or met with careless misapprehension, is one of those minor trials which secretly gnaw feminine fortitude. The subjects which so tormented her filled his mind too, it seemed. Whenever they met, they soon turned to these topics pregnant to them with meaning. They fanned in each other's hearts their discontent and envy over which, I have said, the evil spirits which dwelt within them had already clasped hands. As was but natural, the man's influence, being that of a certain culture, was far the stronger. He lent her books which, between the enforced tasks of her household, she read with strange avidity. He would come of an evening and, while Joe puffed his stump of a pipe on the porch, under the pink lamp-shade,—already, alas! grown spotted and soiled,—their heads bent close, Oakes would explain to Mrs. Bush intricate passages. The books were all in the same strain. Strong pleas against authority, cries of revolt, protests against tyranny and oppression, statistics of unutterable cruelties, crimes, miseries, stern facts about a groaning multitude while a few feasted; a bold scoffing at all religious teaching, shifting kaleidoscopes of horror and despair; above all Reason, with its Ego, which will be heard and satisfied; the individual unwilling to be flattened in the mortar of humanity, mocking at patience. From the perusal of these works Beth rose tottering, uncertain, bewildered; a gradual loosening of all her old faiths, a slow but sure deletion of all her former beliefs went on in her soul, which seemed to shrivel within her. Her teacher was too young and too inexperienced to appreciate the peril of sowing such seed in such a soil. By a gradual disintegration her wish to rise was giving way before his dispiriting forebodings of general destruction. She felt within her the rumblings of a distant, brewing, tempest. Her arm was a strong one; could it accomplish nothing? The sense of a hopeless doom enveloped her. Sometimes at night it laid a cold hand on her heart. In the meanwhile Joe, having said a short but fervent prayer, lay on his back, snoring loudly, enjoying the repose due to the just.

"What do you think of Mrs. Bush?" Mr. Marston had asked his wife, after the first interview.

"I don't make her out exactly," said Lola. "She was rather pretentious and dressed up for a farmer's wife. Americans are so absurd in such matters. I confess I liked Mrs. Daggett better. She didn't put on airs."

"O, she was well enough, but old Dag was such a brute of a drunkard. It's just as well his last spree killed him. This man seems steady and honest. I rather want him to stay; so if she has crotchets, conciliate them a little, my dear."

"Why, I'm sure, darling," said Mrs. Marston, "I'm always nice to servants. By the way, there is already some row. The domestics say she snubs them, and refuses to be on visiting terms. There's been some fuss with Pierre."

"What difference can that make? There was too much running too and fro in Daggett's time with the men and maids. I didn't like it. If she's reserved, so much the better. There'll be less gossiping."

"And she's quite dissatisfied with the cottage. Says she wants a new kitchen and veranda, like ours." Mrs. Marston laughed.

"O, well, perhaps this autumn I'll put out a small wing for them. It is cramped; and while the builders are here I don't care if they knock up a piazza for her at the east of the house."

Mr. Marston preferred expense to personal trouble.

"I'll tell her what you say, Archie. Perhaps she'll be more contented."

There were always men at work upon the place. They were now putting up an elaborate fence to divide pasturage from woodland.

Mrs. Marston, remembering her husband's words, signified to Mrs. Bush upon the following morning that she would again receive her. Beth once more put on her paraphernalia of war. It was now the blue gown and the sailor hat. She burned her front lock off with the tongs, which it is to be supposed did not sweeten her temper or improve her appearance.

Thus shorn but not baffled, she was ushered into the library. This lofty apartment always seemed somewhat over-furnished and encumbered. There were too many chairs, too many bookcases, too much bric-a-brac, entirely too many lamps, which were overtall and overshaded. Lola never felt quite at home in it. Indeed there were many parts of the house whose decorations delighted her husband, but made her uneasy. They fretted her eyes with their elaboration, their lack of repose. More poetic than artistic, she lacked, however, that individuality of taste which finds an instant remedy. She was sometimes a little helpless amid her splendors.

Mrs. Bush found her in a high-backed gilt chair, her feet on a velvet cushion, reading. She wore a peignoir of some flexile texture, rose-colored, cut in Greek fashion, with flowing sleeves slashed at the shoulders, displaying her slender arms. It was bordered by bands of rich creamy Valenciennes laces, clasped at the throat and waist with buckles of pearls. On her fingers sparkled many splendid gems. Her head was crowned by a large black hat surmounted by dusky tufts of ostrich feathers. Her eyes were deep as quiet lakes sleeping in shadow. Asch was lounging on a stool at her feet, but scrambled up at Mrs. Bush's entrance and escaped.

All the old worship which Beth had once felt for this woman while still unknown, and which more recent sentiments were quickly stifling, now woke within her. A healthful admiration for her loveliness suddenly mastered her.

"You look just like a picture, Mrs. Marston."

CHAPTER IX

Lola blushed. " Really? " she said, smiling, " you are very kind to tell me so, Mrs. Bush, if it is a pretty picture. Sit down here by me. I want to talk to you."

" You look just like you used in my dreams."

" Your dreams? "

" Yes," went on Beth, catching her breath and with a nervous twitching of her hands. " I dreamed about you before ever I saw you. I'd read about you for years in the newspapers."

" O, those dreadful newspapers! "

" They ain't dreadful to those as lives dull lives," said Beth, forgetting all her former Pontifex boastfulness. " They bring 'em into life."

Something in her hurried utterances arrested Lola's attention. She had not guessed her to be dramatic.

" I never even look at those things about people. I don't care much for that side of life."

"No, you *live* it," said Beth.

"And I can assure you, Mrs. Bush," went on Lola, laughing, "that it is much more amusing to read about, and sounds much nicer than it is. A great deal of it is a horrid nuisance."

"Mr. Oakes says," said Beth, "that the rich say that to keep the poor quiet, to keep 'em grinding and sweating, while they dance and make merry."

"Ah? Mr. Oakes?"

"Yes, he's a young gentleman as visits us here."

Mrs. Bush's momentary naturalness gave place once more to her artificial "company" manner. Her mouth pursed itself. Her tone became prolonged and nasal. Her backbone snapped into rigid line.

"A friend of mine. He's real smart. He reads with me evenings. He's teaching me the mandolin."

It is hoped that Lola's heroic efforts not to laugh outright, a desire to which the exact imitation of her costume had already given wings, was not evident. She made a grimace behind her hand to recover the equilibrium of a sufficient gravity before replying.

"O, yes. I've heard of him. He's very nice-looking. He has queer ideas, has he not? I heard he was leaving here on account of them. That he was a . . a . . socialist—or something."

"He only took the place just for a while until he got suited." Beth's vocal organs were more and more languorous. "He ain't at all like the people around here. He's above 'em. He says the socialistic doctrines will soon invade the world."

"Dear me!"

"You ought to think him nice-looking, Mrs. Marston, for I guess he admires *you* very much.

A few days before, Oakes had asked Beth's permission to read aloud to her an original poem which he intended to set to music for the mandolin. The verses were addressed "To Lola," and were a painstaking imitation of De Musset's "Andalouses," of which its author had lately made an exhaustive study in the original. Oakes, with praiseworthy industry, had taught himself to read French. The opening words of the love ditty were, "Pale as an autumn night."

"Why, that's quaint! It's Mrs. Marston's first name," Beth said suspiciously.

"A mere incident—it's a common enough Spanish name," the schoolmaster answered.

Then they had spoken together of Mrs. Marston, and Beth noticed that the sneer which met her mention of every member of that high-life circle which so filled her with curiosity, and which she so envied, had died on his lips. He had said little, but Beth, who was observing, made a mental note. She expatiated to Oakes on Fenno Asch's incredible impoliteness, not only to herself but to Mrs. Marston.

"He ain't civil enough to bow to a woman if he goes by her, and he don't know enough to open a door for her."

And then with energy Oakes had again applied to him that epithet of "bull-calf," which secretly delighted Elizabeth.

"He admires you very much."

Lola was quite serious now. She could hardly recover her speech, so disconcerted and nettled was she. Why this woman was quite too dreadful.

"I'm sure I'm greatly obliged to him, but I hardly fancied he would be so . . . presumptuous." She rose and walked to the window.

Beth saw she had committed some fateful blunder, and a purple flush dyed her brow, which the burned lovelock left lorn and exposed. In a moment Mrs. Marston had turned around again.

"I sent for you this morning, Mrs. Bush,"

she spoke in a business-like voice, "to say that I mentioned to Mr. Marston about those improvements over your way, and he consents. The new piazza will be begun next week—the kitchen, later."

Beth, who had never known before such comfort as she now enjoyed, and who had almost forgotten her request, opened her eyes widely, and could only murmur her thanks. Mrs. Marston hoped she would go, but her visitor still sat on the edge of her chair, embarrassed, fidgeting, caught in the difficulty of the departure whose mesh tangles the uninitiated. Lola was beating an impatient tattoo on the parquet floor with her high-heeled shoe. The situation was becoming intolerable.

"Will your family visit you? Do you expect them here?" she asked at last, in a dry, staccato voice.

"I wrote my sister-in-law and her husband," said Beth, recovering her composure, "to come up Tuesday. I guess they'll be glad to. They ain't been married long."

After a few more questions about her relatives, she did finally get herself out.

"She's entirely a new experience," said Lola that evening to her lord. "I doubt if they'll do."

"Why, how?" he asked.

"O, she says such extraordinary, such unsuitable things to me. I can't make out if it's ignorance or impertinence."

"A little of both, I should imagine," said Fenno Asch. "I met her on the road this morning. Whew! She looks a vixen!"

Lola lay back on her cushions and laughed.

"You can't imagine—the funniest thing—I nearly fell off my chair when she came in. She has exactly copied my old blue gingham, and wore a hat just like mine. She looked like a guy."

"What sort of things does she say?" asked her husband; but Lola did not tell him.

As to Beth her whole mind was in a ferment. Her speech, which Mrs. Marston had rebuked and now forgotten, burned her as with a hot iron. "Presumptuous"; she looked up the word in the thumbed dictionary she had used at school, to make sure she was not mistaken. Should she tell Oakes—brand him, too, with this insult? Then there were evidently mistakes as to the laws of fitness. Why did Mrs. Marston wear soiled cotton gowns of an afternoon at five o'clock and appear so splendid of a morning? Why did she read when other women worked, and work when others read? Was it true what she had said that the life she lived looked sweeter than it was? To Beth it looked very sweet. To Beth the Marstons' library, with which fastidious critics found fault, was an apartment of imposing and unparalleled magnificence. Her vanity, which somehow this woman's mere presence seemed to excite and fan only to grind to dust, rallied a little at the thought of her sister-in-law's impending visit. Before Mary Bush, now Mrs. Bucknell, she could pose to her heart's content. The word was unknown to her, the attitude was becoming clear. She could dazzle her at least. There had been no lamp-shades in Pontifex, Dottie had been decked with no locket and yellow ribbons, there had been no vase of roses, and, beyond all, no Mr. Oakes. She planned, and plotted, and arranged how she could at once startle and petrify the Bucknells with the glories of her present lot. It was Wednesday—they would not arrive until the Tuesday following—and this gave Beth five days in which to prepare her *coup*. Again on Thursday she had herself carried into town. This time she went alone. She could not be troubled with the child. She took a horse-car from the crowded ferry, and was jogged across the city to the precincts of Sixth Avenue. Here she alighted to walk. One after the other, she passed the shops of dry goods and novelties, ribbons, lingerie, and the mysterious product known as "neckwear." She reached finally one whose dimensions and importance seemed to suggest what she required. She was speedily at the dress-goods counter. She spied a piece of rose silk crêpe-de-chine in the niche behind the clerk's head which satisfied all her longings.

"How much is this a yard?" she asked, fingering eagerly the clinging folds which he unrolled before her.

"This comes expensive, ma'am," said the clerk. "It's four dollars."

"Four dollars! And only single width! Why, it's terrible high!"

"That's so;" the clerk gave an impersonal shrug. "There's cheaper cashmeres in the same shades at the next counter."

"Show them to me, please."

They were much coarser, thicker, more opaque, and still very exorbitant in price. She hesitated for some time, but at last recklessly came to terms. This dress must have a train, and she measured two extra yards for the flowing sleeve. Then there was the lining, two yards and a half of pink ribbon, and the lace! At the thought of the lace her courage flagged. She priced a piece which she admired lying on a pile of tulle. The clerk informed her it was five dollars a yard, but, seeing her dilemma, presented her with some at sixty cents which he said would do for summer wear. Upon Mrs. Marston's tea-gown there had been fully a dozen yards of a very different quality from this cheap stuff. Even Beth, who could not distinguish real lace from imitation, felt convinced. She compromised by buying five yards.

"It ain't needed on the train," she said to herself.

The next few days were employed in the fabrication of a Greek garment such as should make Mary Bucknell's eyes dart from their sockets and her mouth water. She hesitated about the bare arms. Hers were very dark, rather thin, and there was down on them. No, she did not dare. Not before the men, the farm-hands, her husband. Blind as she was, she did stop short here. It could not be risked. She filled the interstices with white muslin. The effect was peculiar, but she thought passable. She had also purchased a wide black hat, and she surmounted it with two high plumes, as Mrs. Marston's had been surmounted by a half-dozen, and a bow of ribbon. It was more becoming to her than the sailor one. During these preparations the cottage meals were more or less irregular. One night Dottie and Joe went to bed supperless, and it is certain that Joe churned the butter and saw to the hens.

Beth, in poking about the cowhouse one day after some eggs a vagabond hen had hidden there, caught sight of an old gilded harness hanging on a peg, evidently discarded by the coachman. Its meretricious glitter caught her fancy. She came home and indited a carefully written letter to Mrs. Marston in which she asked permission to use this harness with the family carry-all. She got Mr. Oakes to correct the grammar and expression of her screed, and when it was completed it was worthy of Madame de Sévigné. She signed it "Mrs. Elizabeth B. Bush." Her messenger, the shepherd-boy, returned with a brief word scratched across a card. It told her hastily that she was welcome to the harness if it was all right with the coachman, as Mrs. Marston knew nothing about it. This was signed, "Truly yours, Lola Marston."

For nearly an hour Beth pondered over this missive. Was this the sort of letter grand ladies wrote to each other, or was its curtness a fresh slight especially directed to herself? Then there was the signature;

this certainly was friendly,—"Truly yours, Lola Marston."

In a note to Floribel Pullen she signed herself, for the first time in her life, "Beth Bush." It was hazardous, but at all events she would risk it. She was burning her ships, and concluded that whatever she did would be wrong. A certain audacity seemed the safer mean.

Floribel Pullen gladly accepted her invitation to supper. Beth was torn between her desire to exhibit Miss Pullen to the Bucknells, and a slight dismay at the thought that the Bucknells must be shown to Miss Pullen. Azubel, the brother-in-law, was not elegant.

"My sister-in-law's real plain," she said to her at church on the Sunday. "I can't say as she's dressy, but they're used to the best society down in Pontifex. They're old-fashioned, but they're used to comfort and going with the best."

Mrs. Bucknell's plainness, she felt, could thus be made to appear mere eccentricity, a vagary of an otherwise distinguished person. In this aspect it became a distinction. For Azubel she felt it wiser not to apologize.

Floribel had felt a little left out in the cold during Mrs. Bush's and the schoolmaster's philosophic studies. She herself was not philosophical. She liked fun, flattery, and to be made love to. Percival Oakes found Elizabeth's tremulous uplooking held a charm which Floribel's comradeship had lacked. His and Beth's vanities, which were not frivolous, were more successfully complementary. They had something better to do than to make love.

The golden harness was duly polished, and did service bravely over the farm team. Joe mopped his brow, put on his Sunday coat, and went to the station to meet his relations. When they reached the cottage, after their hot drive, the sound of music agreeably titillated their ears. As they entered the parlor this was the tableau that met their surprised glance. Sitting on a tall chair with a cushion behind her, and another under her feet, was the lady of the house. On her head was a large hat, surmounted with nodding plumage. She was dressed in strange garments, flowing and rose-colored, trimmed here and fastened there with lace and ribbons. At her feet, in a recumbent but slightly cramped position, sat, or rather crouched, Mr. Oakes. He was picking at the mandolin. His performance was occasionally interrupted by the sound of sobs and screams from the upper floor, the evident protest of a person in pain. It was in fact — Dottie.

Ten minutes before the *entrée* of her relatives Dottie had broken the only flower-vase, spilling the water over her best dress and yellow ribbons, and scattering its roses pell-mell to the carpet. By turns indulged to excess, or severely disciplined by her foolish mother, Dottie was an exceedingly disagreeable little girl. She had willfully and disobediently pushed the table near which she had been forbidden to play. She was now paying the penalty of her crimes in bed, undressed, and locked up. This unlooked-for *contretemps* had rendered the tranquil and ideal scene which met Mr. and Mrs. Bucknell's astonishment a trifle difficult, but Beth was learning to surmount dilemma.

CHAPTER X

Lola Marston often left her gay guests to their own pastimes in the long evenings, and escaped from them to the upper air of her balcony. She would linger here for a while, glad of a few brief moments in the soft summer air, glad of the rest from their jests which sometimes wearied her; of their merriment, which sometimes jarred. She would lean out and gaze across the wide plateau to the woods beyond, whose dim outline rose unreal and shadowy under a myriad stars. The smell of the dark orange trees, the glimmer of the statues, the vocal melodies of air and nature reminded her of Italy, where she had spent some years of childhood. She liked to draw into her lungs the acrid perfume of the leaves, the distant odor of the tides, which blew across the marshlands. She liked to lose herself in the soft lapping silences, in the cool stillness of the dusk. She was a little tired—tired of talk, of badinage, of light.

Oakes, passing by one night, skirting the

grove of locusts, through which a path had lured him from his direct homeward way, looking up, saw her. The rules of etiquette were not well known to this intruder, and yet a form of pride, akin to finer instincts which guide the civilized, had thus far guarded him from willing trespassing. · Far down within his soul he knew full well that his assiduous visits at the cottage sprang from a secret wish to be brought nearer to the mistress of the castle. He had ceased to desire to see Mrs. Marston. He desired that she should see him. Recognize him she must, admit his existence, be forced to know he had a name, his own name, not some other man's. This curious obsession is less uncommon than we imagine—this passionate craving for a place in the regard of one who represents a world apart from us, beyond and inaccessible. Her approval, at least her notice, had waxed of infinite importance to the phantasies of his sick mind. Her world! how far from his! And why? He ground his teeth when he remembered how small he seemed to it, fit only to be trodden into insignificant obscurity. This longing to-night had grown into positive pain, and when he saw the distant flutter of her draperies he boldly struck the footpath which came so nigh the house that he could hear the music from the open drawing-rooms.

Should he speak to her? make some excuse for loitering here? Coin some false phrase, invent some wily subterfuge that should, for a moment, make her bend her head in his direction, or mayhap whisper a word to him across the night? But when he was indeed so close, a step upon the gravel, a sigh, almost, would have revealed him to her, his courage sank. Trembling, ashamed, he cowered against a tree-trunk, hidden amid the bushes, fearing to breathe lest her unconsciousness should be disturbed.

Away in the distance the Italian gardens slumbered. The roses nodded sleepily; great, high gladioli shot heavenward, the mignonette threw out its dank aroma, while yellow lilies exuded heavy savor, in which the bees sank swooning. The dancing nymphs gleamed like fantastic specters amid the shroud of vapors, which hung low on the fountain. The marble basin glittered between its dusky borders, while its waters dripped in ceaseless cadence. Across this peace, the shrill and tender cries of birds, piercing or plaintive, awoke a dissonance like some regret, some black remorse, clutching the conscience in an hour of pleasure.

The phlox waved purple clusters, white

petunias drank the dew, the amarantus slept in its wet leaves, the nebulosa looked like smoke-flecks upon the verdant borders of the pathway. The garden lay asleep with its stiff hedge-rows, its cut yews, its quaint dwarf birches. The philosopher in Percival Oakes's heart gave way, the poet awoke. He glanced upward—he saw her at last in all her glory, this pale lady of his musings. She was in full evening dress of opaline satin, her arms and bosom bare; above her brow there rose a jeweled coronet. He could guess all her beauty in that white fire which, ever since that day when she had thanked him for a service, seemed to environ her. What mental phenomenon was it which made this unknown woman to this unknown youth a thing to be at once worshiped, pitied, and adored?—for in his feeling for her there were tears. Sterile as death, barren in its unearthly purity, his ideal passion yet was warm enough for him to resent that she should suffer. And . . . she suffered. Had he not guessed it? Why should she not? Love's own avatar! Why was she left to lonely reveries on nights like these? Why was she not missed and swiftly sought for? What were her thoughts, this lady of the gentle eyes? He guessed that they were sad. The Madonna in glory, robed with clouds, her slender feet upon the crescent moon, immaculate, serene, could not have seemed more unapproachable than she did now. Afraid, he slunk away, hugging the bank, and was soon lost in the fast-gathering gloom. Clouds swept the firmament, a chill crept up the valley from the Sound. Lola shivered and sighed, as if some angel of sorrow had brushed her with its pinion.

"How cold it grows!" she said.

She came back into her room. She took up a candle, and shading it with her hand as she crossed the windy hall, went in, an instant, to look at her sleeping son.

"Darling angel!" she whispered, as she bent beside him. She drank in the sweet breath from between his hot red lips. It was like nectar to her. "Darling angel!"

The sadness in her face vanished. It gave way to an ineffable content.

They claimed her when she appeared at the drawing-room door with a round of applause.

"Bravo!" cried May Plunkett, who was spending the night at Marston Terrace, "I've won my bet!"

"What bet?"

"Mrs. Ayrault insisted that my last *risquée* story had shocked you, and that we would not see you again to-night."

EAT NOT THY HEART

"Why, I did n't hear it," said Mrs. Marston, smiling faintly.

"I said . . ."

"Stop!" said the rest. "Do you wish to drive Mrs. Marston away again? It is not decent in her own house."

"What geese!" said Mrs. Marston. "If you are all still quarreling, and as noisy as when I left you, I will surely go away again, and to bed this time."

May Plunkett was leaning back in an armchair, her bright beauty in the full bloom of its twenty years.

"She puts us all out," Mrs. Ayrault said with a laugh that ended in a funny little groan.

Lemuel Isham, whose presence was made audible by a wheeze and roar—his cough resembled the protest of an angry lion—was sketching her.

The old artist's steady eye and hand, with only a bit of charcoal, in masterful, broad strokes had already thrown upon the canvas a silhouette of unusual force and character.

"That won't do—that won't do. Hold on . . ." he muttered to himself. "That will all have to come out. Why, I 'm spoiling her! I 'm giving her a soul!"

"What did you say, Mr. Isham?" said

Miss Plunkett, raising her head from a whispered colloquy with Asch.

She was the only girl he ever deigned to notice. Why he did so was enigmatic. She was an heiress, but Asch did not seem in a hurry to make matrimonial investments. He preferred his friends should do so. There was less risk, and Asch was essentially prudent. This was one of the occasions when he was indulging her. Duly grateful, she did not wish to loose a moment of his attention.

"I said," growled Isham, "that it was impossible to do you justice without color —without the flesh."

"You said nothing of the kind. Did he, Mr. Asch?" she asked, coquettishly.

"I should say . . . the flesh was very important, don't you know," said Asch, fastening his eyes upon May's throat with an impertinent stare.

The girl flushed, but the man's senses remained as cool as a mountain brook. Perhaps it was this unruffled calm before their charms which piqued and pleased the women. Who can tell? It certainly was more convenient. Nineteenth-century women are too much occupied for complication.

Old Isham took off his spectacles and looked at them both. He blinked.

"You are actually growing fat! too fat!" said Asch. He had a thin, membranous voice, highly pitched.

"Thanks for the compliment," said May Plunkett, piqued. "I've just lost eight pounds. I was weighed in the Turkish bath."

"Where did they go—the eight pounds?" asked Asch. "That is what I always ask myself. What becomes of 'em?"

"What becomes of dead birds?" said Mr. Isham.

"Eh! What the deuce have the birds to do with the eight pounds lost by Miss Plunkett? I can't see."

"Whew! whew! whew!" Mr. Isham went on working, his nose within two inches of the easel. "No, I dare say not."

"That is queer," said May. "I never thought about that."

"Have you ever thought about anything?" asked Mr. Isham.

Fenno Asch threw back his head and emitted a loud laugh utterly devoid of mirth.

"Why, Mr. Isham, how horridly rude you are!"

"I'm not half as rude as your friend, Mr. Asch," said Mr. Isham. "I don't think you too fat. On the whole, I rather regret those eight pounds. If you say so, I'll put them in here. The question is, to what part of your frame do you wish them added?"

"Mrs. Marston," cried May, "come and take my part. The gentlemen are behaving cruelly to me. They are making fun of me and saying nasty things."

"O, I think you quite capable of self-defense, May dear." Mrs. Marston was looking over some music at the piano with Count de Beaumont, who had been torturing a sonata of Beethoven's ever since dinner.

"Ah, *voila*, we hold it," said the Count. "Hum, hum, hum."

"'*Adieu Grenade, ma charmante.*' They sang it in the Champs Élysées. All Paris went crazy."

"Hum, hum, hum. Is that it?" asked Mrs. Marston.

"Not exactly. Yes, now. Hum, hum. We've got it. *Parfait.*"

"Well, here goes then." The two mingled their voices while Mrs. Ayrault drummed the accompaniment.

"That is too high for me. My voice is such a poor little squeaky thing. Can't you transpose it?"

"I'll try," said Mrs. Ayrault. "There now, begin again."

Tum, tum.

"'Et le doux son de la mandore
  Frémissait sous les doigts légers.'"

"That is just like your fingers, so smooth and so light," he found time to leave in her ear, between the couplets. Mrs. Ayrault improvised a running interlude which she ended with a crash.

"They can be heavy enough," she said, shrugging her shoulders. "But don't you think we've 'punished the piano,' as May says, with our improvising long enough."

"No, no. Go on, go on. It's perfectly lovely."

"'*Adieu Grenade, ma charmante*,'" hummed May, joining in the refrain.

"It's a dream! Is it not, Mr. Isham?"

"I don't know anything more invigorating, unless it's Mr. Asch's conversation," said Mr. Isham.

Asch glared at him, scowling; but the Bostonian went on drawing, imperturbable. Asch's mere voice acted upon his nerves as does the barking of a weak-lunged dog when one wooes sleep. It must be confessed, however, that Asch's bark was not persistent. He had the genius of pause.

"How much longer do you suppose Beaumont intends making an ass of himself?" said Asch.

"How an ass? He sings delightfully," said May, teasingly, wishing she might rouse jealousy.

"Why, with the Ayrault and—generally"

"You cannot comprehend such devotion, now can you, Mr. Asch? A man giving his whole life—for—"

"Rot!"

"That's just it! You think all love rot!"

"Well, isn't it now? Did you ever see any that wasn't?"

"I'll wager she never did." Had Mr. Isham sneezed or spoken? "Whew! whew!"

"Were you ever jealous, Mr. Asch? I don't mean a little, but murderously."

Asch opened his handsome eyes in a wonder which was at least sincere, but he could find no word.

"You seem to think all the—er—emotions rot," said May. "Did you ever experience that one?" And she giggled. But Fenno Asch's genuine astonishment at her surmise still robbed him of speech.

"I do so love a jealous man!"

"Women always do love donkeys!" said Fenno.

"You are right there," said Mr. Isham, with an unmistakable accentuation. "They *dew.*" He rang out the last word in the best Nantucket twang with which he sometimes amused the ladies after breakfast.

"So you think a man's a donkey for being jealous? I don't. I respect him for it. I even love him, for in that way one can torment him so nicely."

"Thanks! I'd rather be comfortable."

"Ah! You do think jealousy uncomfortable?"

"Can't say. Never tried it,"

"Then you have never loved!"

"Shouldn't be surprised," Mr. Isham mumbled as he gave a sharp pat to May's charcoal eyebrow. He rose, and made from a distance an exhaustive examination of the portrait.

"All wrong; all wrong. It's got to come out! There's too much sense in it. Might be a Santa Scholastica. Why, there's actually some expression in those eyes. They're not foolish enough—irresponsible. It's all got to be done over. I've spoiled her. Dear me! dear me! The limitations of art are incredible."

"And you, Mr. Isham, have you ever loved?"

"Ah! my dear Miss Plunkett, I was born too soon. In my day, to be in love was a great expense; and you see I never could afford myself the luxury."

"Why—I don't understand!"

"In those simple, frugal times, to love meant marriage," and as May Plunkett moved away to speak to Mrs. Ayrault, who was calling her, the old man went on as if addressing the ambient air. "Girls did not have *dots* in those days, and men had to earn their own living. Their greatest happiness was to slave for the worshiped lady, to bestow everything upon her, for which, in return, they felt themselves blessed if she gave into their keeping her little hand. To-day fortunes are a heritage; love an investment. I am old. I leave the field to the more enterprising generation." And he waved his hand toward Asch with a contemptuous inflection on the word "enterprising."

"Do you know, Mr. Isham," said May, who had caught the last word, "I think the old fellows are more enterprising than the young ones. They are less . . . er . . . prudent." She looked at Asch as she spoke. "But I missed all that you have been saying. Tell me over again."

"I was saying the boys had to rough it in my day, dear young lady; and that prudence was not a part of our valor."

"I hate prudent men," said Miss Plunkett. "Cowards are prudent. But what did you say to Mr. Asch?" she persisted.

"I must not repeat myself," said Mr. Isham, smiling and shaking his head, "although that is one of the prerogatives of age. One would not like to become a bore." He sighed.

"Fancy your being a bore, Mr. Isham, with all your wonderful talent!"

"What has my talent to do with it?" asked Mr. Isham, gruffly. "When did society care for performance? All it wants is personality. It asks us to be ornamental, amusing, or amused; and it is quite right, too. The bores are those who expect its praise for the things it cares nothing at all about. For the things of which we are most proud, our friends rarely give us credit or applause. Now, I do not want the applause of society. How could I growl and bark at it if I owed it gratitude? Society is a tonic. It kills our vanity. It shows us its folly. Nobody cares for our best actions or our best gifts. When I was a very little boy I saved the life of a friend's pet dog, but I got my jacket and my hands dirty, and I remember that my father whipped me severely. He represented society which dislikes the unsightly."

Perhaps Mr. Isham knew that it was his very bark and growl which made him acceptable, and he could laugh in his sleeve at the human masquers who found his own disguise piquant.

In the other room a quadrille had been formed. Of course nobody knew how to dance it. Its formality had degenerated into a general scamper and frolic. A couple were playing backgammon in the library as a cover to sentiment. Others had strolled out upon the terrace. From one to another of these scattered groups Archibald Marston wandered—the amiable entertainer, the genial host. Never, perhaps, had the realization of his ambitions been more absolute than to-night. He had at his house to-day the very cream of a coterie famed for exclusiveness. Fashion was represented by youth, beauty, and wealth, but in his character of man of the world this was not enough. Isham was there to do the heavy artistic; de Beaumont, diplomacy; there was even a stray congressman out on the veranda, admitted because politics was to him a fad, not a career, and he was chatting with a young married lady who had once been known to publish a sonnet in *Harper's Magazine*. Even literature was not neglected. It is doubtful if any of the house-party had read the sonnet. They spoke of it vaguely, in whispers. It is also quite certain that had they read it they would have criticised it with unusual severity, seeing the author was their intimate companion. There are no more severe critics of an art than those who know not its alphabet. At the time of its publication there had been a moment of terror, followed by a reaction. They generously decided not to drop her. For this there were four reasons. She was pretty; she dressed extremely well; she was good-natured; and she gave amusing little dinners at which "frumps" were never met. Would she have "frumps" after the sonnet? That was the question which agitated the community for six months. One never can be sure. Sonnets are proverbially upsetting. The first year settled the question. She did not change her circle. She was saved!

Yes, Marston was happy—perfectly so! There was the house. It was the apple of his eye. He was careful not to appear too well pleased with its stately proportions, its luxurious furnishings, but he could with difficulty conceal his satisfaction under a well-bred indifference. Above all he was pleased with his wife. She certainly was exquisite. How superior to all these fussy, restless women whose languid manner was mere affectation, disguising petty aims and low designs. *Her* indifference was not feigned. It was real. Sometimes, indeed, it had vexed him—vexed him that she was not more modern, that her conservative ancestry had left with her traditions which made her resemble a mediæval lady of the sixteenth century wandering bewildered through the noise of this. But to-night, as he looked at her, he appreciated that this was power. He realized in her that something which raised her above them all—nay, above him—and he felt generously inclined to forgive her! He went now and touched her arm, and said an affectionate word to her, so overbubbling with his pride that he did not care if it was "bad form." She instantly responded with her soft lips pouting out at him; behind the raised top of the grand piano her palm sought his, and she gave his hand a gentle little squeeze, a glow of tenderness lighting up her sweet face. He was not often so demonstrative.

The party was breaking up. It was nearly one o'clock. The moon hung low on the horizon; the clouds had drifted away. The night was superb.

"It is quite too beautiful to go to bed!" said the author of the sonnet, coming in nevertheless, with her congressman.

"I really must disappear," said Mrs. Marston. "I have to get up early in the morning, and drive very, very far. I shall leave you to your own devices, and to Archie's."

"Where are you going?" they all asked.

"O, no matter! You could never guess." And she would not tell them. She was, in fact, going to pay a visit to the county poorhouse, which she never neglected, however onerous might be her other duties.

CHAPTER XI

The poor house—a square, brown building, surmounted by a cupola—stood at an angle of two roads in a pleasant field. It was surrounded by trees. Although over its low doorway one might well have written up the "Lasciate ogni speranza voi che entrate" of the great Tuscan's hell, yet its aspect was not particularly forbidding. It was only when one penetrated among its tenants that the sense of its gloom struck a chill to the heart. Although Mrs. Marston had the habit of visiting "Smith's Institution," as this refuge was called by the courtesy of amiable trustees, she never did so without the inward shudder with which we face an unwelcome task. When the effort was over, she heaved a sigh of relief hardly tempered by that sense of exhilaration which the priests tell us duty done leaves with the virtuous. What satisfaction indeed could come from the contemplation of such hopelessness?

To-day she found the inmates already at

their midday meal. In the summer they had a light supper; in winter the meals were reduced to two, and they went supperless to bed, the fact that the evenings were shorter being given as excuse for this curtailment.

Lola was too sincere to indulge in that foolish exclamatory admiration with which the dwellers in luxurious homes view hospitals, asylums, and retreats dedicated by charity to the unfortunate. Nevertheless, so strong is the force of custom, that even she was not quite free from that forced cheerfulness, that strained approval with which the children of the world accost the children — shall we say — of the earth? The painful contrast of her elegant garments with the squalor of their own humbled her into that apologetic attitude with which the man who occupies a seat in a drawing-room car nods to his friend who is hurrying to find one in the rear. Yet it would never have occurred to Lola Marston to change her manner of dress to suit this new environment. In this she was wise. It is best always to be one's self. There is nothing to gain—and least of all with the uneducated, whose force of vision we should not undervalue—by shams or by hypocrisy. She knew they liked to see her as she was, and, beyond this, being in spite of her softness a person of individuality, she did not purpose to suit herself to others. She demanded that they should suit themselves to her.

The matron met her in the upper hall. She was a disheveled woman with a ruddy, coarse complexion and a somewhat abrupt manner. She was not unclean, or entirely ill-favored, however, and under her turbulent and vigilant defiance there lurked, Mrs. Marston knew, a sort of shamefaced sympathy for the beings whose welfare she was delegated to watch over. She showed Mrs. Marston into her room. Two decidedly dirty little children frolicked on the floor. One, a charming little girl in a soiled scarlet frock, ran up smiling, and touched Mrs. Marston's rich coat with wonder and delight. The other, a robust boy of three, scrambled up into a rocking-chair, having possessed himself of a greasy picture-book. In his mouth he held a long rusty iron nail; now and then he took it between his thumb and index, and puffed out his pink cheeks.

"Well, if he ain't smoking," said his mother, with sudden laughter. "He sees the old men a-doin' of it, and he's such a monkey he just catches up all he sees."

Mrs. Marston smiled.

"They are dear children," she said. "What are their names?"

"Keziah and Johnny, ma'am. After me and my husband."

"Ain't papar comin' in to see the lady?" asked Keziah, stroking gently Mrs. Marston's lace parasol.

"O, I guess he'll be along," said the woman, whose name was Mrs. Monk.

"I have never seen your husband," said Mrs. Marston, with the same set smile which gave her jaw a feeling of having been dislocated and reset.

"He ain't much to look at, but he's good; he's a year younger 'n me," said Mrs. Monk.

"O, that makes no difference. You're young too," said Mrs. Marston.

"Well, I ain't so young as I was. I'm going on thirty."

"And how are they all?"

"Much the same. Old Madam Kate's gone. We had her funeral last week. Mr. Walsh, he came over to read the service."

"And Mrs. Davis, is she still here? She seemed such a hearty creature. I should think she might get work."

"Well, and so she could." Mrs. Monk leaned back in her rocker, displaying her thick feet, swinging far apart gracelessly, in their woolen socks and stout shoes. As she rocked she caressed the end of her nose, upon which the heat had left its flush, with her knitting-needle. Her garments exuded that curious odor which do those of persons whose effects are washed in the same place where their cooking is done, and as Mrs. Marston looked at her she found herself wondering how any man could love this woman, or even want her—this woman in whom all element of charm seemed so entirely absent.

"About Mrs. Davis—I have to laugh!" Mrs. Monk rocked vigorously, and indulged in a peal of hilarity. "She'd got a splendid offer, only six weeks back. A widower—two sons—wanted her to look after them a bit—do the cleanin' and mendin'. Five dollars a month—all found! Well"—Mrs. Monk tipped her chair and laughed again—"well, she wouldn't quit here. She's in love!—and it ain't with the house neither."

"Mrs. Davis? That old woman?"

"You may say it."

"You're joking, Mrs. Monk?"

"No, I ain't. Ask Maggie."

Maggie was the wit of the establishment; an Irishwoman, irrepressible, with a wagging tongue and a shrill jollity which reverberated ever and anon through the silent halls.

"In love!"

"I guess that's the color of it. She's just crazy after a man here. Amos P. they call him. His name's Amos P. Hubbs."

"Mr. Hubbs!"

"Well, if it ain't queer, I don't know."

"Why? What?"

"Says she knowed him when she was younger, over in Brooklyn. That may be. I must say them two is n't like the rest. They're educated and quiet-spoken—and, well, I suspect they've been better off. She washes for him, mends his pants and duds now and then, does little chores for him. He ain't no good. He's got the rheumatiz. But he's a great hand to talk. Well, he hangs around her, and they're dreadful set on each other."

"That old woman!" Mrs. Marston could only ejaculate again.

"Yes. He ain't so old. He ain't more'n fifty-five, and she's goin' on sixty if she's an hour; but she's a fine-lookin' woman for all that, is Mrs. Davis, and that widower would have hired her. Well, would you believe it, she weighed it in her mind for two days and nights. She could n't sleep or eat—she was that flustered. It meant leaving the poorhouse, and she's a well-born woman, Mrs. Davis, and a good home, and wages, too, agin' a rainy day; but when the time come she could n't do it. You see she could n't leave Amos. I guess she thought he 'd kinder miss her."

Mrs. Monk laughed once more, but this time there was less spontaneity in the merriment; it wavered a moment and then ceased, sobering into sudden silence. Mrs. Marston, too, had grown grave.

"Is she quite alone in the world—quite friendless?"

"She ain't got no relatives as I know of. They 're all dead, or maybe ungrateful. She 's been a good woman always, so I heard some folks who knowed of her tell. Nobody ever asks for her. She 's been here nigh on seven year. Her husband was a bad egg, I guess, but he ain't livin'."

"Then I suppose this . . . er . . . affection . . . is the only one she has in the world."

"Well, I guess it 's all there 's left to her."

The last words were uttered in a tone so gentle that it was almost a sigh. Mrs. Marston looked up surprised. Her deep eyes met the opaque ones of the matron. There was a pause.

"The quaintest thing is she 's changed religions. She was Congregationalist—Mrs. Davis—blue as blue! Went to meetin' reg'lar. Yes, a reg'lar blue light. Well, will you believe it, when the priest come here to see Amos, when he thought he'd die with pain across his chest, three weeks back, she ups and gets him to baptize her a Catholic. Now, ain't that droll? I guess they'd like to be married, but we could n't have it here."

"No!"

"I don't say as if they went out and did it as the trustees could raise objections. There ain't no law agin' marriage. But you understand . . ."

"Yes."

"Well, she's bound to be the same as him. I guess she was afeard if they wan't the same religions they'd get separated somehow in another world. They ain't got much to look for here, I guess."

Mrs. Monk's voice was a little husky.

"So this place has its idyl," murmured Lola.

"Eh?"

"Its love affair."

"Seems so."

They were silent.

"How sad!" said Mrs. Marston, after a while.

"Well it is, now you come to look at it." Mrs. Monk stopped, and scooped up her son who had crawled to her side. She buried her face in his tangled curls with a maternal gurgle of satisfaction.

"She isn't so unattractive after all," thought Mrs. Marston, with contrition.

A sound of moving chairs warned them that the diners had finished their repast. In a few moments Mrs. Marston entered the women's department. There they were all, Maggie and Phœbe and Mrs. Davis, with her added aureole of romance. Her handsome motherly face smiled under its black fluted cap. Maggie was obstreperous as usual, full of gossip and reminiscence, teasing the others, and shaking her old yellow face at them.

"Have done, Maggie Sullivan! You're crazy. Here comes a lady."

There was Phœbe, the ruddy giantess, who had lived all her life in the poorhouse, and had borne a child there, so long ago indeed that, though the girl remained, the scandal which had heralded her birth was half forgotten.

The girl, Tot, stood now with arms akimbo, idle, dawdling, simpering, upon the neighboring door-sill. Tot was not "all there," as the Scotch have it.

Then there was Diana. Diana was a negress. She was as black as ink. O, Artemis, starry-eyed, swift of foot, would not thy lip have curled in scorn and anger had this namesake of thine dared pollute thy great Ephesian temple, seeking blessing?

About Diana there hung a horrible and ghastly interest. Even Mrs. Marston found it difficult when the wretched creature was in the room to detach her eyes from a fascinated scrutiny of her shapeless, ghoulish ugliness. She was short-limbed and heavily built; from her swarthy throat her head rose, unnaturally small. It was perfectly round, surmounted by a crown of bristling wool; her forehead was flat and lowering; her nose wide; her jaws prognathous, with brutal lupine lips, which held between them always the stump of a clay pipe. The ratlike roving of her beady eyes suggested a mind preyed upon by impulses of malignity and apprehension.

"When she ain't smoking she gets fidgety," the matron here remarked. "Gets sort of wild and nervous, and can't do her dishes."

At twenty Diana had been nurse to the child of a farmer's wife. One day furtively she carried the child into the neighboring woods, and there crushed in its head between two stones. She had no dislike to the baby — no grudge against its parents. What savage and sensual instinct found vent in this hideous deed? What inherent depravity was known only to herself. The jury had disagreed; six were for hanging her, while six insisted she was irresponsible. The word which the slayer of a President has left to us, that crisp and comprehensive appellative "crank," had not been added yet to our American vocabulary. That word which designates those dangerous beings who vacillate forever upon the edge of madness was still to be invented by one of its most virulent exponents. Diana was refused at the Lunatic Asylum, declared unfit for the Idiot's Home, so twenty years before, she had been brought here. There had been talk of a new trial, but time, perhaps, had assuaged the grief of the bereaved mother; at any rate, here ever since she had remained, forgotten. If the furies which had shaken her youth still slumbered, who could say? She passed her days in washing dishes; if now and then she rattled them in the sink, nicking their corners with vengeful emphasis, it was perhaps the expiring protest of a burned-out volcano. She always curtesied to Mrs. Marston, calling her by name, but with her Lola could never bring herself to speak, acquitting herself by a nod of greeting.

To-day her attention several times wandered to where a new physiognomy detached itself from among the well-known ones of the women. Something there was, however, of reserve and modesty in the bearing of the new inmate, so that she hesitated to intrude even a smile in her direction. Her tact was rewarded. The young woman, who was neatly dressed and had a certain refinement about her person, moved forward and addressed her.

"I'm a newcomer, ma'am," she said. "I would never have been here only for my child."

"Ah!" said Mrs. Marston, her eyes all sympathy.

"Yes, I had a good place down by Roslyn. They're rich folks. I scrubbed and cooked for the men in the lower farm. The lady was kind to me. She let me have Rosy. Rosy's my child. But one day her arm began to swell up, and she got the blood-poisoning, and I had to leave my place to nurse her. She came near dying. The doctor says I saved her with my care. But they got a Polish woman, and she did not have any baby, and so . . . I found it convenient . . . to come in here. . . . I had to come."

"Why wouldn't the widower's place do

for her?" asked Mrs. Marston, turning to Mrs. Davis with an inspiration of helpfulness.

"O, they're decent folks," said Maggie. "They'd take no young 'uns."

The young woman flushed, and made a deprecating gesture. Mrs. Marston turned the subject which seemed to involve some hidden sting, and continued to chat with the others. Rosy's mother relapsed into silence. By and by she left the room. In a moment she reappeared with the child in her arms —a lovely child with dark curls, great lustrous eyes, and cherry lips. The little one had on a clean cotton frock.

"This is my Rosy," she said.

"Surely, surely," said Mrs. Marston, kindly, "she doesn't look like an invalid. She's a beauty."

The mother's face lighted with pleasure.

"Does she now?" she said. "She's nearly well."

"Are you English?" asked Mrs. Marston.

"Yes, ma'am. How did you guess?"

"By your speech," said Mrs. Marston, "as they said to Peter."

"Well, I won't deny my nation, as he did," she answered, a trifle proudly.

"She is very intelligent," thought Mrs. Marston. "Oh, how dreadful!"

"You see," said the young mother, while a bright pink color rose in her cheeks, "she's the best baby when she is n't ill. I used to tie her with a long rope to a tree just outside the window where I worked so I could see her, and do you believe she stayed there all day long with never a whimper. Just laughing and crowing and playing by herself. I used to carry her milk out to her. Those people were good. I'll never get such another chance again. People won't have children."

"She's a lovely child," repeated Mrs. Marston, with that sense of despair such cases awaken in us.

She noticed that her words found no echo with the other women. She rose and made her adieux, leaving a golden coin in little Rosy's hand.

Still, on the whole, with all their lack of charity, with their frivolity and narrowness, the women imparted something to their surroundings which the men could not. Somewhere within those withered breasts there were movements of motherhood, love-tones, an occasional spark of that lightheartedness which God has given to feminine things, — that spirit of natural gayety which bubbles up now and again in the veins of the most sorrowful of women, a flotsam of their girlhood. There were plants in the window where they sat; there was even a canary-bird in a wooden cage, singing in the sunlight, and they themselves were occupied. Many of them were sewing, and all were chatting. If it was not home-like, it was at least not grave-like.

But grave-like was the melancholy of the men's ward. Two or three tramps belonging to that genial genus which perambulates country roads, and whose stomachs are always ready to absorb cold griddle-cakes, discarded biscuits and warmed-over coffee, sat near the door. One with crutches, one in a high, brimless hat, one in a tattered uniform, were exchanging a monosyllabic colloquy in a corner by the empty stove—which served as a spittoon. These were the men of the world. They had something to relate. But the others, the others! Each alone on his chair, his back to the wall, unoccupied, humiliated, undone. With the fine perceptions of her delicate nature, Mrs. Marston noticed that this humiliation—this sense, as it were, of mortification, defeat, failure—which left no mark upon the women, had stamped itself indelibly here. They avoided her eye, they had nothing to say. All was over! She had brought some newspapers, and she now produced them and tried to rouse their interest in the last election.

"Well, ma'am, I was once a Republican," said an old man, rising and offering her his seat. "And I'm an old soldier, and I got my pension, but I'm so sick I came in here for the doctor. I'm eighty-three and full of pains. I guess my pension'll not last 'em much longer."

"We gave 'em a good lickin' this time in the State," chuckled one of the tramps, addressing no one in particular, and rubbing his knees. He was "Crazy Jim," who scoured the country roads early and late. A hump-backed man, with an embarrassed manner and a pinched, starved face, appeared at the doorway. "That's Mr. Fussi. He's a musician," said Mr. Hubbs, addressing Lola.

Fussi, too, was a new arrival.

"Are you an Italian?" asked Lola. His pathetic figure filled her with pity.

"My father was," he replied, shortly. He had one of those faces which haunt the memory.

"And you are a musician?"

"Whose music nobody wants," he said, with a smile that Mrs. Marston never forgot.

"Good-day." Flourishing one arm as if

he were uncovering before her, the musician turned away and went quickly up the narrow stairway, vanishing from her sight.

"He's a perfect gentleman, Mr. Fussi is," said Mr. Hubbs. "But I guess, like the rest of us here, he's met with misfortune."

"Well, I'll bring you fruit and oysters the next time I come, and I hope you will all be well. Good-by, Mr. Hubbs."

"Good-by, Mrs. Marston."

"Good-by."

Once more in her carriage she could think again. It was a ten-mile drive through woody lanes and meadow lands. The sunshine lay upon the fields. Summer breezes ran with crackling sounds through the dry grass. The mill at the old pond turned lazily its crumbling wheel. The thirsty cattle drew close to the water under the shade of trees for shelter from the heat, switching their tails to brush from their dry flanks the flies that bled them. Their lowing and the buzz of insect wings were the sole sounds which shook this scene of infinite repose. Yes, she could think, and there was time. Think! What did it all mean? What were these wrecks of the world? Why were they ever born to linger thus? And were they really as miserable as they appeared to her? Self-love protected them, perhaps. We are never, in our own estimation, quite as forlorn as others see us. But to Lola all was pain, and to her useless questionings the only answer was, as she drove homeward through the quiet noonday, her silent tears.

CHAPTER XII

It is difficult to remain on any height. The bluest sky breeds tempest.

A cloud appeared athwart Archibald Marston's visual ray as he threw open his shutter, and looked down on his fair terraces early one morning. This cloud was found to be somewhat larger than a man's hand. It was also found to be of a vivid crimson. Under close inspection it proved to be of mousseline de laine and to assume the outline of a woman's polonaise. It obscured, to him at least, the entire horizon. Because of it he could not eat an egg the butler brought him, nor drink his coffee with appetite. After this unsuccessful meal he returned to his window. Yes it was still there, flagrant, indecent, insolent.

Upon his terrace, not thirty feet from columned portico, there was a stone seat, a favorite one with his guests, many of whom could see it from their windows. Upon this seat, arrayed in this peremptory, harsh, cruel color—it was of that magenta red which gives the toothache—sat Mrs. Bucknell, and by her side, in black, not red, this lady's husband.

He rubbed his eyes, did Mr. Marston, to be sure he was not dreaming. But no, they were too real. There could not be a doubt. He told himself that they would linger but a moment, that it was a mistake, some horrid blunder they would speedily repent of and be gone. But no! what did he now perceive? She rose and spread a shawl down on the grass, on which she squatted. She pulled some worsted from her pocket, she began to knit, while Bucknell, stretching himself at full length upon his stomach on the seat, pushed back his hat between his ears and began to sleep. Before assuming this attitude he had slowly removed his shoes, which lay on the grass near to his wife's knees. His large brown cotton socks rose between Mr. Marston and the view.

Ringing hastily for his valet, Mr. Marston gave him to understand that there were some strangers in front of the house, that they must be at once informed that it was inhabited, the grounds private, and that they must . . . er . . . move on . . . or, rather, off.

The valet speeded to fulfill his mission. He found Mr. Bucknell too sleepy to disturb, and therefore addressed himself to

Madame. He came back shaken with laughter, hardly able to assume that decorous demeanor which Mr. Marston exacted from domestics. When he recovered speech, it was to say that Mrs. Bucknell had informed him that they were no strangers, but friends, the sister and brother of Mr. Bush, and would do no damage. They continued to snore and knit. Mrs. Bucknell even turned around, and from under her big bonnet grinned and waved her hand at Mr. Marston, while the valet delivered her message, as much as to say:

"It's all right. We are all one family. Don't worry. Ta—ta!"

Mr. Marston was transfixed. Hurrying into his dressing-gown, oblivious of his bath, he almost ran across the hall and tapped at the door of his wife's apartment.

Lola was having her hair combed by her maid before the mirror. Her husband's wild uncomeliness gave her a start.

"Why, my dear, what is it?"

"Come!" he said. His eyes were glued to hers with an ominous glitter like a snake's charming a bird.

"Come, why, where?" asked Lola, still more mystified. But he continued to beckon with one finger and to repeat, "Come!"

Hastily tying the ribbons of her white

robe de chambre, her hair upon her shoulders, Mrs. Marston followed her unshaven husband. He almost pushed her to the window, where from behind the curtain they watched the Bucknell pair, still sleeping, knitting, and immovable.

"Well!" said Mrs. Marston, with a short gasp.

"It's a picnic!" said Mr. Marston. "I think they've brought their dinner. They evidently mean to spend the day, possibly the night. Mrs. Ayrault's windows open just here, do they not, my dear?"—his voice was unnaturally pleasant and urbane—"and Ackley's, and the Count's, and others? Oh, yes, Mrs. Sanford's." (Mrs. Sanford was the author.) "Pretty sight, is n't it?"

"Have you sent out?" asked Mrs. Marston.

"Yes, I've sent out. I sent Marvin. And they did n't go!"

"They did n't go, Archibald?" said Mrs. Marston, tragically. "I've said this all through, and you would n't listen."

"'All through?' What are you talking about, Lola?" Mr. Marston paced the floor impatiently. He was certainly not handsome. The sense that he was not at his best, but at a disadvantage, increased his irritability.

"That Americans would n't do."

"Nonsense! What has 'Americans' to do with it?"

"They don't know their place. They are impossible. I ought to have insisted."

"I say nonsense!" Mr. Marston spoke with that sharp, short anger of the habitually amiable. He was in fact exceedingly annoyed, not exactly with his wife, but with everybody who might be about. I once saw a child fall and hurt herself. She ran across the room and slapped her brother's face. Humanity's revenges are not more logical. The Anarchist who cannot kill the God he defies, curses and slays his creature man.

"If they don't know their place they've got to learn it. Of course I won't put up with this thing a moment longer. I'll have Bush sent in and either dismiss him . . ."

"He is such a nice man," said Lola. "So sweet and patient over Archie's garden. Ackerman never would plant it in rows as he wants; and children like to carry out their own little ideas, and I think it's a good thing. It makes them self-reliant; and then Daggett did drink so, and Joseph is quite sober. He works early and late. He is very industrious. Daggett was frightfully lazy."

The magenta polonaise fluttered on the wind.

"O, of course, my dear, if you *like* this hugger-mugger style of living with chumps like these eating clams on our front piazza steps, I have not another word to say. Perhaps you wish to ask Mrs. Bush to dinner to-night, or else we'd better turn this into a tramps' lodging-house at once."

Mr. Marston's sarcasm was lost on his wife, for her head was out of the window.

"She's got on the queerest sort of a bonnet, and Archie—heavens!" Mrs. Marston gave a muffled scream. "He's got his boots off! You didn't *tell* me *that*, and she's nursing them! She's got them in her lap!"

Mr. Marston drew near with the face of one led to execution.

"You'll have to go down, dear!"

"Just as I am?"

"Without one plea!" laughed Lola.

"I'll be damned if I do! I beg your pardon, my dear, but really . . ."

"Then *I* will," said Lola. She knew her husband well. She knew he would fume and fret, but when there was anything to be done that required moral courage, she did it. There was a reason for this. True moral courage braves opinion. Herein lay all the difference between their characters. Mr. Isham had guessed it. It was one reason why the satire which he could point so mercilessly was never directed at Mrs. Marston. He addressed her always with deferential courtesy, listening for her answer with respect.

Fortunately, the Long Island mosquito, just then borne on a gust from the falling tides, blew inland, and began to whiz, and buzz, and sting, about the head and face of the reposeful Bucknell. From their post of vantage Mr. and Mrs. Marston watched the attack, saw Mrs. Bucknell's waving arms charge in gallant defense, smiled at her final slow but sure defeat. The crimson lady stumbled to her feet, picked up her shawl, folded her knitting, shook her slumberous lord, not over-gently, gave a parting scowl— the sun was in her eyes—at the colonnade and the offenders, unconscious of their misdemeanor, pattered down the steps.

Lola heaved a sigh of relief. "But it's only put off," she said. "Of course, somebody's got to speak to Bush."

Notwithstanding his Anglo-Saxon dislike of "scenes," anger did sometimes give to Mr. Marston a force which in milder moments was unknown to him. Physically he was as brave as a lion, morally he was a poltroon.

Enough occurred on this unfortunate day to let loose the dogs of war, and of his wrath. Later, while walking in a portion of his woods especially reserved for his family's uses, he caught sight of a man and woman sauntering leisurely before him. Their heads were half concealed by a blue parasol, the woman's gown trailed in the leaves. Yes, it must be his wife. His wife and the Congressman, to whom she had promised a stroll about the place. He called. They stopped. They turned. They faced him.

"Ah, how are you, Oakes?" he said in his bland tones, as of a good king to his subject, from which the other shrank as from a blow. "How are you, Mrs. Bush?"

"I'm pretty well, I thank you; and you, Mr. Marston?" said Beth.

"So, so. Pleasant afternoon, isn't it?"

"I don't seem to care for the climate here," said Mrs. Bush. "It ain't anything like so cool as Pontifex."

"It's entirely a matter of taste," said Mr. Marston, who wished to be disagreeable, but did not know exactly what measures to adopt. "I should advise people who do not fancy Long Island to live elsewhere. In fact to avoid it. They can be spared. Ha! ha!"

There was no mistaking his meaning; and before Oakes! Elizabeth trembled, blank with resentment.

"Good afternoon, Mr. Marston," she said, shortly, and walked on. Oakes followed her with a gloomy bow to the master, his step weighed with import. At the same time his anger was more directed against Elizabeth than against Mr. Marston. Too entirely devoid of humor to gauge her follies and laugh at them, the young man was not lacking in certain instincts of propriety, which had suggested to him that very afternoon that they should bend their steps in another direction. He had proposed a different walk. Beth had not listened. If he entertained the hope of meeting Mrs. Marston face to face, it was certainly not under such conditions, dancing attendance on her farmer's wife. Of course the growing antipathy between Mrs. Bush and her employers, the tumult of contradictory emotions which filled Beth's breast, the conflicts of her mind, were quite unknown to him. There are those to whom we find it difficult to repeat the unkind comments they inspire. If this springs from some special personal dignity Percival Oakes possessed it. Beth had never dared reveal to him the words with which Mrs. Marston seemed to degrade him. No, she could not! Therefore this intrusion upon the lady's grounds was the more excusable. Nevertheless, unsophisticated in such matters, ignorant, he had protested, and now the whole unwelcome situation suddenly dawned upon and sickened him. Before a man belonging to the class that he abhorred, he had been placed in what a false position! And he owed it all to her! As he looked now at the thin outline of her mouth, and watched the nervous clutch with which she grasped her parasol, he thought her hideous. In fact, for a moment Beth had become so. That he should have lent himself so long to her persistent claims upon his time may seem peculiar, for after all he was far, far above her. His restless, ardent mind had wider ambitions than hers, for she thought only of herself and of her child; he harbored hopes for the race. Yet it perhaps was not all mystery. Hidden agencies work subtle spells. Percival Oakes was young. He was not wise. He was alone in the world. He was conceited, egotistic, arrogant in spirit, but he was loving. It is not easy with all these attributes to be a stoic. It must be remembered that if he had no happy, joyous outlet for his affections, he had no impure one. He lived chastely. He had no mistress, and no sweetheart. The vine-embowered cottage, the bright lamp, the cheerful tea-table, the enthusiastic welcome of a very handsome woman, who dressed for him — he knew it — who listened to his words in rapturous admiration, who was zealous to learn all he could teach, whom he felt to be no ordinary person, dizzied his brain a little, not overmuch, but a little. It was the nearest semblance to a home that he had ever known. It stilled in some mean measure his hunger of the heart. There was nothing else. Floribel Pullen amused him. She never interested him. Beth was interesting. Her longings, her aspirations, her dissatisfactions, her complaints, nay, her very asperities, raised her to quite a different plane from the giggling schoolgirls and cackling dames of Paradise. Floribel Pullen had laughingly told him that he came to see her so rarely now, she was sure " handsome Mrs. Bush " was cutting her out, and he had felt a slight pleasure at her chaffing; but to-night he felt no pleasure. A brutal desire to revenge himself on the woman beside him for this encounter with Mr. Marston, and the latter's contemptuous parting exclamation, led him to say just the one thing which in her sorry plight Elizabeth could least support.

" I saw Madam Marston driving yesterday," he said, in a dogged voice. " I thought her the most beautiful woman I ever beheld. Pity she married that fool."

"I had heard about Mrs. Marston before I seen her," said Beth, trying to steady her voice, whose tone was indistinct and hoarse. "When I did meet her I was n't so much struck with her beauty. She ain't exactly what I'd call a reg'lar beauty."

"Oh, there are beauties—and beauties," said Oakes, clearing his throat, taking long swinging strides, and slashing at the leaves mischievously with a stick he had cut. "There are coarse, showy beauties, and there are others like tall lilies that look as if they'd break if you breathed on them."

"Oh, I guess Mrs. Marston's tough enough," said Beth, with heightened color, "for all the training and ramping she does from morning to night, with all the comp'ny they keep." She laughed a trifle shrilly. "Why, Joe says they ain't to bed most nights until near morning." Her devouring curiosity about the doings at the "big house" had led her to frequent nocturnal catechisings of her long-suffering Joseph.

"These grand ladies," said Oakes, "have the obligations of their position." He stopped short, amazed at his own Philistinism. How unmercifully he would have sneered at this phrase if launched by another.

A flood of jealousy, not bred in the flesh, not born of passion, but none the less fierce, implacable, ran riot in an instant through Elizabeth's throbbing veins—one of those pristine, savage torrents, which no mortal can foretell, no moral effort quench. The enmity of sex to its own, old as the universe, which, in spite of priest, and prayer, and invocation, still sways the human creature, swept her, resistless.

Had Oakes half understood his influence on this woman, the impression and power of his words, their full significance to her, it is certain that with all his boasted iconoclastic theories, he would have now been dumb, have ceased to fan her animosity; but he was self-absorbed, young, inexperienced. He therefore continued to exasperate Elizabeth with foolish praises of Mrs. Marston's loveliness.

"Miss Pullen is one of them coarse beauties you speak about, perhaps?" she said, ironically. "But the people here say you like her very much, that you're real intimate with her." She looked at him narrowly, with eyes that threw out blind sparks, like a cat's in the dark. She had lingered on the word "intimate."

Oakes raised his eyebrows, shrugged his shoulders, and remained silent. He lacked the breeding to indignantly defend Floribel from intended aspersion, yet was not quite disloyal enough to sully her.

"Why don't you stand up for her?" cried Beth, lashed to fury by his calmness. "It's dirty things the folks here say of her and them as dangles after her. If I were a man —or half a one—I'd die before I'd let a lot of foul-mouthed witches throw mud at my ... my ... sweetheart, and say ... and say ... I shared her love with other men who was richer 'n me, and winked at it."

She ended almost in a shriek. Even before he had abruptly touched his hat and left her, without a word of farewell or of warning, she realized the enormity of her assault, and that it leveled her in his regard with the lowest of her kind. The vulgarity of her speech, its uncalled-for violence, its disgusting familiarity—unknown to men and women of her class, be it said to their honor —and the comparison he would draw forever between her and ... that other one—not Floribel—upon whom all her rage now centered, against whom he might guess her words were aimed, filled her with infinite despair. In losing him she lost the one higher link between herself and that refined and graceful atmosphere she so much coveted. Was it her fault she was not educated, gently nurtured? Was it a crime her youth had been so hard that it had left its harshness on her features, its roughness on her hands? But now she had put herself outside the pale. She might rail against the inhabitants of Paradise, calling them her inferiors, might boast to him, as she had done, of her insulting slights to Mrs. Marston's servants, to Mr. Rose, but now he was a prince, Pierre Rose, compared to her—she was a fish-wife. One of those bare-legged, unsexed creatures that dug for clams down on the shore, in tattered sunbonnets, with bony arms, and scraping shovels, who swore and quarreled with each other, and stopped to drink at the liquor-seller's on their way home. She staggered into the cottage, and fell upon her face, across the sofa. Her breast was rent with dry and tearless cries.

CHAPTER XIII

By and by her moanings ceased. She picked herself up from a recumbent to a sitting posture; she smoothed out the crumpled breadths of her petticoat with that habit of thrift and of order which is not easily unlearned. Economy of work, that lesson poverty teaches, made her regret the carelessness which would necessitate the smoothing-iron. She began to pull at the flowers in her hat, whose edges had been crushed in her abandonment. She dusted its edges with her handkerchief; then, pressing this to her burning eyes, she sat down again as if to gather her scattered faculties.

Now, Elizabeth was a clever woman, albeit undisciplined and lacking in soundness of judgment, and already in her heated brain the thought was uppermost how to reinstate herself, to regain her scattered self-respect, to return at least to where she had stood before. At the mere memory of Oakes she shuddered. For the first time she comprehended the exaggerated space he had occupied in her horizon, the exalted importance she had attached to his opinions, the almost febrile interest with which she had listened to his oracular discourses, his impractical denunciations. Sobered by the occurrences of the afternoon, remembering but too distinctly Mr. Marston's words, remembering too, the home from which she had come, to which she doubtless must return if she left this, her better, wiser self, not penitent, perhaps, yet humbled, warned her to pause, to examine herself well. Such systematic self-examination had been a part of that religious training which the puritanical influences of her childhood fostered. It was not unknown to her. Suddenly the mysteries which environed her seemed rent. She saw with physical distinctness a downward path, intoxicating yet pernicious, to which her steps were tending. We often run with astonishing heedlessness down a hill, which we know must be reascended, and it is only when we have nearly reached the bottom we stand aghast at the distance stretching behind. Many, discouraged, remain in the valley; they have not limbs or wind for the return, but Elizabeth's limbs and wind were not yet exhausted. No perversion is immediate. There are no sudden sins. The soil is rotten. The final crumble is opportunity.

She looked about her.

What a heaven of peace was this little house, how snug, how pretty, how dear! She remembered her enchantment when in those early days of spring it had first met her view. How well in health they had been here! Dottie, herself, and Joe. Joe—with compunction she now remembered how small was the time she had given to him lately. He had been indisposed one day with a slight feverishness, and she felt vexed at giving up her lesson on the mandolin with Mr. Oakes because her husband lay upon the sofa in the best parlor while his room was being swept and aired. She had been cross to him, chiding him for imprudence, for sitting out on chilly nights without his coat, contracting malaria, and giving trouble through his own folly. Then . . . Dottie — where was the child now? Surely, surely, it was her supper time. She had not exactly neglected Dottie, but she too in all these new exactions of dress and entertainment, in all these trips to town, and readings, and Spanish madrigals, had been sometimes in the way; once or twice forgotten. Then the money! Beth grew pale when she remembered all the money she had spent, and . . . on herself, her finer underclothing, her dresses, hats, shoes, stockings, gloves, and the parasol with lace upon it! Joe's wages had been stretched, nay overdrawn. There was a bill she could not meet this month. She had not liked to tell him of it lest it should worry him.

"Dottie, Dottie," she cried, with this new rush of contrition upon her, a sort of homesickness to find her child and clasp her for an instant to her breast. She ran toward the door, "Dottie, Dottie!" As she reached the sill her husband crossed it. Something in his face arrested her, breathless, upon its threshold.

Mr. Marston, when he left Mrs. Bush and Mr. Oakes to finish their twilight ramble, was not in the sweetest of humors. His temper, it might be surmised, was only a trifle less ruffled than theirs. As he crossed his lawn he caught sight of Joe working in the vegetable garden. He quickened his pace and was soon near him upon the other side of the hedge. Stooping over some roots he was conscientiously digging up, Joe raised his head at his master's summons.

"Here, Bush, here."

Wiping his hand on his forehead, and throwing down his trowel, Joe in shirt-sleeves, with his old straw hat rammed down over his ears, prepared to respond.

"Ay, ay, sir." He slowly stepped through the furrows with the measured step of the agriculturalist, which is never accelerated, nor would be though the heavens fell.

"Here, come through the upper gate. I'll walk up and meet you. I want to speak to you." Obedient, Joe turned northward. In a few minutes the two men stood side by side in the open field.

"What are you doing?" Mr. Marston's annoyance had cooled a little, the exercise having increased his heart's action, but he was angry at having to be angry. Such details bored him.

"I was diggin' up of them roots."

"A waste of time for you. Let Charlie do that. It's mere child's play! Did n't I tell you I wanted the hay taken in? There's thunder in the air."

"The hay won't get a-wettin'. Don't you be afeared. There won't be no wet spell at present. I held on to hitch up after loam for the farm road. Farmer Taft's got a fine lot, sir, and it's a short haul. There ain't no rain comin'. It's looked that way every night for three weeks. The drought's on us. I knows it. It won't let up on us yet."

"When I say a thing's to be done it's to be done, you hear, and not to be neglected for something less important," said Mr. Marston lashing himself. "I don't want explanations or excuses. I'm sick of them."

Joe stopped, astonished. He was unaccustomed to being so addressed, unless indeed, by his wife. He was himself so patient that he rarely provoked others, and his wife's "tantrums," as he called them to himself, hardly counted. He had learned to bear them or escape from them with equanimity. "She's kind of excitable," he would say, apologetically. "She don't mean the half she says." He supposed all women to be alike, and their words to mean little. His mother had a high temper too. His experience of the sex was limited.

"I tries to please ye." His eyes, full of melancholy, dwelt for a moment on Mr. Marston, who turned away his own, uncomfortable under their pleading scrutiny.

"I know—I know," he said, more kindly. "But there are things that don't please me —not at all—not at all; which must be spoken about, and it's deuced disagreeable, I can tell you."

Joe pushed back his hat and grunted some inaudible protest. Mr. Marston lowered his tone to a confidential key.

"This morning my wife . . . I . . . we . . .

when we looked out of my ... her ... our windows ... hem—upon the terrace, saw some persons ... er ... a man and a woman sitting close to the house, taking their ease. He had pulled off his shoes. Mrs. Marston was greatly shocked."

"I guess it must have been my sister Mary and her husband," Joe smiled, broadly. He was relieved. He had feared his work did not suit.

"Exactly; it *was* your sister, so my man Marvin tells me. She had on a most extraordinary dress." At the memory Mr. Marston's anger of the morning returned and he scowled. "One which ...er ... made her peculiarly conspicuous to our guests, even from a great, great distance. Such a costume is a blot on a landscape. I really can't permit it."

"Do you want me to speak to her about that dress?" and a quizzical expression rose to Joe's lips. "Her heart's sot on it. Sister Mary never was tasty like Elizabeth— Mrs. Bush, I mean. Allays had a hankering after cryin' colors. Now I never cared for 'em myself."

"Nonsense, Bush!" said Mr. Marston, now thoroughly aroused again. "What have I, what can Mrs. Marston have to do with the accouterments of your family unless indeed . . ." He remembered his wife's animadversions upon Beth's outfit, and wondered if he ought to mention it here. " I mean if they keep out of our sight they can wear anything they please. Your grounds about the cottage are quite large enough for your visitors—quite—" his wrongs whipped him now to say all.

"I'll speak to 'em—to my wife," said Joe. The idea of facing Beth with such a message sent his heart into his boots.

" Really, Bush, your family seem to have no sense of decency, of reserve. Here this very afternoon after the unpleasant—most unpleasant . . . er . . . affair of the morning, I met your wife close to the plateau upon Mrs. Marston's favorite path, with that ridiculous schoolmaster at her heels. He isn't welcome here, do you hear? I won't have him hanging about. I dislike the man. I distrust him. I dislike him excessively. I won't have him on my grounds, and you can tell him so with my compliments."

Joe paled under the tan which made his skin resemble some animal's hide.

" Do you mean," he asked slowly, " that I'm to tell the schoolmaster he ain't to call on us any more? "

" I said nothing of the kind—nothing. I

repeat to you I've nothing to do with your household and its arrangements. You can receive anybody you like unless—unless dangerous characters."

"Dangerous .. ?"

"I'm alluding now to no one in particular. Of course, this is a gossipy little village —so I'm told. So the maids tell Mrs. Marston. I don't hear any of these things. Nor does she, for that matter—Mrs. Marston, I mean. But a young woman as good-looking as your wife cannot be too careful in such a community. With her husband—her child —the dairy, she should have no time for . . . er . . . frivolity."

"My wife ain't ever been the light kind," said Joe, in changed accents. "Nor has any one ever afore accused her of that in my hearin' as I knows of."

The murmur of the thunderstorm seemed to lower near, enveloping them in its heavy breath.

"My good Joseph, no one does now. I'm talking to you as I would to a friend—one of my friends." He made a gesture of his hand toward the house which loomed stately against the sky. There was a pause.

"If that's all you have to say to me I'll quit work now, sir. It's six o'clock."

"That's all." Mr. Marston smiled; but there was no responding smile on Joseph's face. Upon it had descended a settled sternness. He pulled his hat down once again over his ears and eyes, and plodded back into the garden to get his tools.

CHAPTER XIV

"Joseph Bush," said Beth, "what ails you? Is it the chills again?"

Joe entered. He divested himself carefully of his coat, folded it, and placed it upon a chair, but he kept his hat on. They were in the "best parlor," that shaded, cared-for room which had gone through such transformation since Beth first reigned there. Something ominous seemed foreboded by this interview between husband and wife in these official quarters reserved for "company," swept and garnished for days of feasting. Joe sat down by the table, resting his arms upon it, his chin propped by his thumb and index whose dovetail nails sank in his thin jaw.

"No," he said. "I'm some better of them, I ain't got the chills."

"Well, what is it?" His face and manner betokened some unusual occurrence, and there was a kind of desperate resignation in her question, unaccompanied by her habitual sharpness of tone.

Now the messages with which Mr. Marston had charged Joe were not calculated to make him look forward with a great degree of equanimity to this meeting with his wife, and to say that it required all his courage to deliver them—and deliver them he would, come what might—is to state the matter moderately.

"What is it?" There was again a note of hopelessness in her words.

From his somewhat dejected pose he looked up, surprised at her unusual meekness.

"Where's Mary?" he asked, looking about him, weakly trying to gain time.

She remembered that the Bucknells had harnessed one of the farm-horses to the carry-all, and had gone for a drive as far as the mill, taking Dottie with them. They had not yet returned. She told him so.

"Ain't they goin' home Tuesday? he asked, as if preoccupied.

"Yes," said Beth. "Your ma's written the hayin''s on, and she wants Azubel Bucknell back."

There fell a silence. Joe was the first to break it.

"It ain't the chills I've got, but my dismissal, or what comes near to it. Mr. Marston—the master—ain't satisfied."

A purple flush of shame rushed to Beth's brow and cheeks. She stood up before her husband, speechless.

"I guess," went on Joe, in a dull monotone, "I guess he ain't used to our ways nor we to his'n." He looked that she should rant or shriek. Her silence startled him. "I don't know as you've liked it here, though I must say as how we've never had more comforts nor better pay, and the child a-plenty to eat and good air to breathe. It ain't your disposition to be cheerful as some folks is with nothin'. You're terrible ambitious, but I like the place. I thought as how when you was fitted out, and fixed up, perhaps we could save and lay away for when we're old and not so fit to toil. The pay is good. I never dreamed to make so much. Ye see, my wife," he went on, "if you was wantin' to be a lady—I mean to live like them high-falutin ones does over there in the big house, like Miss Marston does—you had n't ought to've married me. I ain't the kind as ever can give it to ye. I ain't a lazy feller. I works and works and works, but I ain't got the hang of it. I can work myself, but I ain't got the hang of gettin' work out of other men. There's them as has it and them as has n't it, and there's no use of cryin' over spilt milk."

The familiar quotation seemed to encourage him, and he raised his head and smiled a little.

"Tell the truth, Joe," said Beth, in a low voice, the crimson flush still on her forehead although her lips were white and dry, "It's me the Marston's ain't satisfied with. It ain't you. You done your work perfectly and they know it."

"I seen my duty and I done it," said Joe, evasively; "but it seems with them highfalutin folks that ain't enough."

"Well?"

"That 'ere dress of Mary's she's so sot on — I bet she's got it on this afternoon — seems she and Azubel went a-traipsing around the big house, and sot themselves right down under the portico, and Mary's dress a-flarin' and —" Joe scratched his head — "the Marstons' comp'ny could see it a mile off, and it wan't suitable."

"Did they tell Mary Bucknell to leave?" asked Beth, with agitation.

"Now, I don't know as they did," said Joe, reflectively, raising his eyebrows; "but Mr. Marston, he says they did n't want any of us to come about their grounds more'n we need.

Beth was strangling, but she gulped down the rising flood of words — where was the use? Mortification at its climax finds speech inadequate.

Joe cleared his throat. The worst was to come, and Beth knew it; but she would not help him. He cleared his throat, but was dumb. He eyed her piteously as if asking her to spare him, or come to his relief.

"There was more he said, and things as hurt me."

"Hurt you?"

"Beth, I ain't been a hard husband to ye, has I?"

Hard to her? He? As she looked at the patient lines about his mouth, and those sad eyes that could not look a lie, and the round shoulders and awkward feet, always so ready to do her errands, a tenderness unusual to her swept her soul. The burning at her heart rose in moisture to her eyes.

"No—no—no—my husband, you ain't been hard!" She laid her hand upon his neck. He took it in his and pressed it gently.

"We've seen good days together and bad ones since we went a-courtin' in your aunt's orchard. Do you remember, Elizabeth? Some of both. I've sometimes thought when Oakes was around, and he and you and Miss Pullen talkin' so smart and lively, as how I'm a rough sort of a chap for such society. I ain't one as is quick like you,

Beth, to pick up ideas. I guess I stick pretty fast to the old ones. Well, I was a-sayin', what with you and Oakes, and your fine dresses, Beth, and all — with my wish to stay here and put by something for ma who is old now and ailin', and worrits with the farm — I ain't got the grit to make a fortune easy — what with it all, seems as if we weren't as happy as we might be."

Something fell and splashed upon his forehead. He looked up at her wonderingly.

"Don't take on so, Beth."

"Did he say anything against me?"

Then heroically Joe said to her: "He don't like you walkin' around with . . . the schoolmaster . . ."

"Well," said Beth, "he can rest quiet. Mr. Oakes and I will do no more walking around, I guess."

Joe was puzzled. She felt almost pleased that a slight was to be put upon Oakes. She wished Mr. Marston had openly insulted him.

"I thought you and he were mighty good friends," said Joe, emboldened. Maybe it's as well to give him the slip a bit. I guess he thinks a heap of himself."

"Yes," said Beth. "I guess he does."

"He thought a good deal of you—eh?"

"Pshaw!" said Beth. Her tears were dry

now. The color had faded from her cheeks and brow. Her heart beat more quietly.

"Well," said Joe, "I guess I'd better go and clean up for supper." He got up and walked to the door. She followed him.

"Joe," she said, "I'm going to try to get along. You told me how it would be before we came. That we'd be little better than their servants. I wouldn't believe it. I will try to bear it for the child's sake."

To this woman death was preferable to acknowledgement of defeat. Since her other methods were deemed offensive and absurd she thought she might regain some status through excess of sacrifice.

"I will do what I can."

He thanked her with a look, and as they heard the carry-all rumble up and stop with its dusty load, the commonplace once more closed in upon them with its inevitable pall.

Mrs. Marston's dove-eyes grew big with approval at her husband's prowess when in his finest ex-cathedra manner he told her of his encounter with Bush.

"I virtually dismissed them if things didn't improve," he said, exaggerating a little.

"Such things are so unpleasant! I'm so grateful to you for taking it off of me."

He continued to boast. He had even attacked the wife and sister-in-law; unpleasant, of course, but necessary. A place like theirs could not be managed without discipline.

She applauded admiringly. "Mrs. Daggett was such a simple person. It seems so odd to have a farmer's wife who needs to be coddled."

"Well, she is very independent. I imagine she henpecks poor Joseph. Of course we need not keep them a moment if they do not suit us. They are only servants after all."

"She hates the idea, the maids tell me. American farmers are not exactly that."

"All nonsense! I pay him—why Rose is a scholar compared to Bush. He speaks several languages."

"I know," said Lola, laughing, "but then he wears a white cap when he is at work. Fancy Bush in a white paper cap!"

The picture sent them both into a peal of merriment.

"The difference is just this," said Lola. "Rose will wear his cap, and so will his son, and his son's son. But Joe's son, if he had one, might be President of the United States. If he took after his mamma he would certainly try to be."

"It's all folderol! That is the reason of all this discontent and dissatisfaction; every boor trying to ape his betters, to do what is not expected of him. Agriculture is as honorable a career as any other, and a far more healthy one. Why in Heaven's name cannot our farmers' sons be satisfied to till the earth, and not be thirsting to be petty lawyers, doctors, and politicians?"

Lola's visual organs suffered a moment's eclipse, in which, on a dark background, loomed a butcher's cart. She only said:

"Dearest, these hopes are perhaps wholesome. This wish for higher education, for a betterment of both men's and women's spheres is robust, and probably vivifying. Such persons are more apt to be industrious and thrifty."

"I don't want people to be stagnant, to remain in ruts," said Mr. Marston. (Had the butcher in some hypnotic current flashed from her mind to his?) "I am always ready to give a helping hand—you know this, my love. Our self-made men are often, nay generally, our best. Some of them indeed, for all we know, may be descended from noble ancestry."

He looked away as if across imaginary continents full of moated granges, turrets, and battlements, and heralded escutcheons, where knights sat at the feet of ladies, coiffed with the hennin.

"Poverty drove some of them across the seas to found families as powerful as the old . . . er . . . but it is false ambitions whose expressions I resent."

"It is sometimes so difficult," said Lola, "to know which are the false and which are the real."

Then he told her there was to be a political meeting in the village soon for the fall election. It would take place out of doors. He had been asked to speak. He meant to take active interest.

"I haven't any particular gift in that line," he said. "But I couldn't refuse."

"I shall be frightened to death if I go to hear you," said Lola. "I thought you never spoke."

"Oh, I'll try not to make a mess of it. I've got through fairly well once or twice at dinners."

Then he unfolded to her his political tenets, to which she listened, dutifully awed.

CHAPTER XV

When Mrs. Marston stepped out on the rickety porch after her visit she was surprised to hear pattering drops of rain. She was also surprised to find it already so dark. Her call, this late summer afternoon, had been upon a neighbor, an humble one, whose cottage lay on the edge of the pine copse, a mile from Marston Terrace. The homeward road was a lonely one. In fact, she would shortly leave the public lane, which was itself unfrequented, to strike into a still more isolated pathway across the woods. She knew she had plenty of time before her dinner-hour of half-past eight—for she was a rapid walker—nevertheless, she was somewhat horrified to find, on consulting the shimmering morsel which was caught by a knot of diamonds on the lapel of her vest, that it was already nearly eight o'clock. She had sat and chatted, regardless of the hour, so rapidly the moments flew in the monotonous droning of old Mrs. Taft's talk. Time passes swiftly when unmarked by shock. She had brought only a lace sunshade, and was shod in light, thin shoes, but she picked up her petticoat, raised the insufficient parasol to protect at least her head and hat, and started off almost on a run. A gust of wind shook her garments. It blew her hair wildly about, whisking short locks into her eyes. She looked up. The clouds were heavy. Almost in the zenith they were black as ink. Now and again they emitted a lightning flash, followed by quick, reverberating thunder.

"One, two, three, four, five, six, seven, eight, nine. If I can count nine between the flash and the thunder it is not so *very* near."

But when she had gone a quarter of a mile she had ceased to count. There was such a confusion of flash and roar that she lost her courage. The inky cloud had burst. It rained in torrents, sweeping the country in its white sheet of unchained water.

"I was a dreadful goose to start," thought Lola. "Shall I turn back?"

It seemed better to push forward. They would be anxious about her at home, and then it would be such a bore. Her gown sacrificed, damp feet, a crushed bonnet, were not irremediable evils. She did not mind the rain and hurricane. The electric currents in the air alone shook her nerves. She gasped a little.

"I'll go on now whatever happens," she thought.

To accept the tempest without struggle brings a sense of freedom and of excitement. She felt no chill; she was in fact burning up with the movement and exercise. She found the path half hidden under its wet oak leaves. Here the pines grew rare, merging into the oak wood beyond. She met no one. One rarely did; the surroundings were rural, not suburban. The few inhabitants of the adjoining farms were peaceable and decent people. There were no tramps so far from a railroad. She had, therefore, no fear of men. She plowed on an eighth of a mile more. Her draperies streamed and dripped. On her cheeks flamed two bright stains. The air was stifling, except when the gusts blew their freshening breath upon her. It was just then there came that terrible experience, that horrible lightning stroke ahead of her, that crash and swirl of terror which left her limbs numb, her hands palsied, her heart cold. One thing, however, it revealed to her. Fifty feet from her was the Dougherty house.

Yes, nestling under the foliage, in its scant clearing, with its miserable green shutters, its peeling walls, one or two forgotten hen-coops overturned at its east end, it rose before her.

"Heaven save me," thought Lola. "I can perhaps find shelter in here. Creep into a window possibly."

She had made sure that she was not "struck," that her limbs were still her own, and not some one else's, and that Dougherty's cottage was a sanctuary of refuge sent to her by Providence.

Dougherty was a poor Irishman, who had suddenly come into an unexpected inheritance. He had been left a farm and some money by a distant relative. He and his brood had hastened to pull up stakes and rush to the seat of their new acquisitions, and the old house with its patch of land was now offered for sale. Mr. Marston, upon a part of whose domain it infringed, was in treaty for its purchase. As she hurried up through the high weeds, which choked the approach, her hand already raised to force, if possible, an ill-locked latch, the door swung open. A man's tall form appeared upon the threshold—

"Don't be in the least alarmed, Mrs. Marston, it's I—Mr. Oakes—Percival Oakes—the schoolmaster."

But she could bear no more. Her nerves

unstrung by her battle with the elements, her hands still tremulous from contact with their fury, she gave a faint cry, and fell back against a tree-trunk, panting, with blanched lips and distended pupils.

"I say it's Mr. Oakes," the voice continued, quietly. "This door was locked, of course. I forced it with my knife . . ."

He came up to her quickly, but she could not speak to him. He, seeing her plight, threw one arm about her, and, lifting more than leading her, drew her toward the open doorway, through which a flood of light escaped into the gloom. She rested her head against his shoulder looking up into his eyes in helpless weakness.

"I have had a great fright," she said, by-and-by, when she regained her voice. "You must forgive me."

"It's I who need forgiveness for adding to your fears." He had now released her, and was standing at some distance from her. He had made a pillow out of his coat for her head, and had installed her on a rude bench cut in pine which was wedged into the wall and projected toward the open grate, resting on a wooden pin. Some cones and fagots were burning on the hearth, emitting fragrant warmth. It was from these the light had shone upon her entrance.

They filled the room with a yellow, resinous vapor. A rough table stood in the center of the apartment; too bulky, perhaps, for the general removal, it had been left to be disposed of with the property. Lately whitewashed, the walls were not unclean, save from the dust of a few weeks' neglect. But the dust of pines, of dead leaves, and of sand is not the dust of cities. It is purple and golden, and perfumed as if blown from flowers. The fitful gleam of the fire cast a mantle of charity over the hut's denuded poverty.

Mrs. Marston noticed that on the table there was a plate, a knife and fork, a flask and glass, some biscuits, an open basket in which was a pile of freshly-caught fish.

"Were you preparing your supper?" she asked, smiling.

Oakes was still standing awkwardly close to the table, looking down at her. The storm-clouds seemed to have left their grayness in his eyes, whose gravity was drowned in shadows. He was still trying to recover from his astonishment; that amazement we feel when our time has arrived at last. But there are joys we fain put off lest reaching us they find us unprepared. Would the grains of this hour-glass filter upon his heart and stop its beatings, or would they sift a respite on the violent emotions that swept him, so that he might speak to this sweet lady such words as fitted place and hour?

"Yes," he said, after a pause, during which the storm, for a moment lulled, seemed to burst out in redoubled rage. It rattled the window-panes, bending the trees until they cracked and groaned as if in pain. "Yes, I have spent all day on the Sound. I generally do on Saturdays when we shut up the school. I go down for a long swim and to fish. I had some luck to-day. I was coming home—the storm overtook me here, and as I thought I was in for a good hour of it, I lighted a fire with some dry sticks I found in the woodshed, and I meant to broil my fish. I was hungry." He talked rapidly. Was it to give himself or her confidence?

"I hope my intrusion has not spoiled your appetite. You seem to have quite a little picnic here." Her voice was weak and wavering still. She was very pale. She had taken off her hat and was tossing up her hair, coiling and fastening it with a diamond-tipped arrow which held its twisted meshes.

"I take brandy and crackers with me when I go for all the day." He reached for the flask and poured a small quantity of the liquid into his glass.

"Will you not moisten your lips with this, Mrs. Marston? It will prevent you from taking cold, from feeling faint."

"Yes, I will. Thanks." She made a grimace. "I hate the taste, but now, there—ah! it does give life. It does warm one. I was cold."

"And your shoes? Will you not come nearer the fire?—warm your damp feet?"

She leaned down and with a deft gesture resolutely pulled off her low high-heeled tan shoes. They creaked on her open-worked silk stockings. They were saturated. She moved her toes about, and, timidly resting her two hands on the seat, offered them to the flame.

He stooped, picked up her shoes, and standing them up on their slender heels on either side of the hearth, watched them a moment as the humidity ascended from them in a tiny streak of spiral smoke.

"Ah!" he said. "They were wet indeed!"

"Give me a biscuit, and do go on cooking your fish. It looks awfully fresh and nice. Who knows—I see no prospect of a dinner to-night, and I have missed my afternoon tea. I may as well have my supper with you. My family are doubtless at this moment dragging the Sound for my dead body, and beating the woods for my remains. Will you give me some of your fish, Mr. Oakes?" She pouted out her soft lips as she made this last request in her own enchanting way.

Without replying he made a rampart of fresh fagots upon which some red ashes had already fallen, and placed the fish across them. They began to broil and sputter. A delicious odor of the sea seemed to rise between the narrow walls.

As he came and went, Lola watched him. His not ungraceful movements, his quick, muscular agility full of that ardor of living which gives the illusion of strength. He wore a gray flannel shirt, and had a blue silk handkerchief knotted carelessly under its collar. He wore knickerbockers, with coarse gray stockings. He had thrown off his sailor's cap. His thick curly golden hair, still moist from his bath, smelled of the brine. His hands, sunburned and knotty, the philosophic hand, had certain fingers tapering to artistic shapeliness. The veins of his brown throat throbbed with the exertion as he stepped hither and thither, preparing the impromptu meal.

A sense of warmth, of security, of comfort, a sort of dreamy spell crept over Mrs. Marston's consciousness, and she continued to watch him at his silent work, her head against his coat, her feet to the heat, her hands about her knees.

"You seem to know how to cook," she said, by-and-by. "My mouth is watering already at the aroma of your cuisine."

"I used to prepare all my mother's meals," he said, "when I was young."

She smiled. "Do you speak of your youth in the past tense?"

"Life is not measured by years always, but sometimes by hardships," he said, shortly.

"Was yours a hard youth?" she asked, softly. He was certainly interesting. The thought of Fenno Asch flittered across her mind.

"My mother was always ill, and we were miserably poor."

"How sad!"

"Yes, I suppose it was . . . sad," he said, with a slight sarcasm in his tone. "Your friends would think so. They call themselves people of the world, I believe, but I guess, Mrs. Marston, they do not know much about it."

"I dare say not."

"She was ill, and she couldn't eat. I

used to make up little messes for her when I was only a shaver of eleven."

"You were a good son."

"Oh, I do not know about that. I was cross to her sometimes. I do not forget it."

"And . . . she died?"

"Yes, she died. Poor woman! The fish is cooked, Mrs. Marston. I'll bring you one." He carried his little plate over to Lola with her fish, some biscuits, and a glass which he had now filled with water—water with which he had provided himself before her arrival, drawn at the well in a rusty pail. She began to eat. He sat down on the floor and ate his own fish as best he could in his fingers, washing it down with a draught from his brandy flask.

"I was very hungry. It tastes good, does it not?" he said.

"Perfectly delicious!"

The rain once more swept the window with its flood.

"And you were very young when she died?"

"Twelve. That left me quite alone in the world. I believe I have some cousins in the West. I imagine they do not care about their poor relatives. Most people do not. I was what is called well-born. My mother and father were educated people. She was the daughter of a clergyman. Not that I care if I had sprung from tramps. It's all the same to me."

"Have you a contempt for all refinements?" asked Mrs. Marston, courageously. She remembered what she had heard of him, and wondered now if he would unfold to her his peculiar views. He was washing his hands in a broken bowl he had found, and wiping them hastily on his handkerchief. He came and stood with his back against the mantel, closer to where she sat. At last he was near her; near that light breath, those soft sighs, the ripples of her hair, the outlines of her mouth, more guessed at than seen in their dim environment, that chaste breast! Those long, thin, white fingers of hers were near! And near was that melodious mystery of womanhood, that personality differing from all others he had touched; that exquisite, intangible aroma of the patrician, of the lady, separating her from other elementary women, making her a creature of another sphere, almost another sex from Beth Bush and Floribel Pullen.

"Have you a contempt for all refinements?"

"Not for such as yours." He must have spoken though she should resent the personal note as insult, and slay him for his boldness. Ah, let her slay him! What matter—the hour was here!

"Mine!"

"I mean," he went on, hurriedly, "I hate the vulgar upstarts who think they can patronize such as I, when I do not ask their patronage, or want it. In you, one feels the real lady. One sees it. I mean, the first time I ever saw . . . I beg your pardon!"

But great ladies are sometimes amused at what unsophisticated persons think will offend them. His allusions to upstarts passed unnoticed, for she could not have believed he meant her husband. Lola did not remember to have passed so odd a half-hour in her life. She was alive to her finger-tips. Her nerves swung back into a reaction of mental activity, ripe for impression.

"What do you know about me?"

"Do you ask me that to remind me of the great distance between us?" he asked, bitterly.

"Oh, how can you think such things!" she cried; but even as she spoke she weighed the distance, and vaguely wondered what her husband would think of this prolonged and extraordinary tête-a-tête.

"I dare say many of my thoughts would horrify you," he said, gloomily. "What I know of you is all naturally in my imagination. I have a little of that. I scribble verses sometimes. They are said to be fairly good." He could not help telling her this. He would have given his life to sing for her "To Lola." He thought it a fine thing. His voice had the ring of conceit in it, which had made Joe Bush declare that he thought a good deal of himself.

"You must send me some of your writings," she said, somewhat perfunctorily, and with that sense of impending weariness which any claim upon one's time or admiration invariably arouses, and which painted itself far too plainly on her transparent features. Fenno Asch did not write poetry. It must be admitted that of the very few things he did do he never spoke. Oakes was disappointed. Floribel Pullen's florid if uncritical enthusiasm seemed almost preferable to this bland invitation.

"Oh, I am more interested in all new movements, in watching the efforts of our unfortunate human race to emancipate itself from the thralldom of habit, from the clutches of smug monopolists, of vulgar demagogues, than in composing poems. When I leave this hole, which will be at the end of the school session, I hope to write on these subjects." There was still the aggressive key.

Mrs. Marston thought, "I could have loved him when he spoke of his dead mother, now all charm is lost."

"Of course," he went on, "my education is insufficient, but a man can learn a good deal from thirty to fifty." He spoke eagerly. "This must be a fruitful period of existence. If I live—I am not sure that I shall think it worth while—I may yet learn something to help my kind."

"These problems which agitate the universe are so profound," said Mrs. Marston, "that one must indeed know a great deal to solve them. It needs a man of genius to find the remedy. He has not yet come forward."

"If he did he would not be recognized. They would stone him to death."

"You take a very sad view, Mr. Oakes."

"Oh, to be supreme for a moment!' cried the schoolmaster.

"And yet you would suppress all supremacies?" she ventured. "Is that logical?"

"They are admirable, but not to their victims," he answered. "But I said for a moment. Just time to readjust."

"He is really adroit," she thought. "Really clever."

"I fear we are all arrogant and self-willed, and it was so intended, Mr. Oakes. The leveling processes that socialists insist upon would cripple individual ambition and paralyze the very progress that they preach."

"That is what the priests tell us," he said, contemptuously, "that everything bad was intended."

"I know so little about such things. I am, I know, very stupid."

"When women have a voice in the conflict it will be heard and felt. You will think more of these things. The time is nigh. I mean to espouse the cause of woman, trampled upon and cheated as she is. You, Mrs. Marston, will know better and care more one of these days for the wrongs of your sisters." He was almost eloquent. As her eyes met his as if in question, he suddenly smiled.

"Why, he has a beautiful face!" she thought. "I do care," she murmured. "I want to help them."

"Do you?" He continued to gaze at her, still smiling, and for some unaccountable reason her eyelids fluttered under his gaze, and she blushed.

"She is one of those women whom no man could betray—betray or forsake," he thought.

"You see I have strange ideas, Mrs. Marston. I look upon the average marriage as upon licensed prostitution," said this very modern young gentleman.

Then, as she did not answer him—"Perhaps you think me coarse," he said. "You must forgive me. I'm not accustomed to speaking with ladies of your . . . class." The last word came forth like the crack of a whip. She bent her head as if she had been struck with it across the cheek.

"I am no prude," she said, haughtily. "And in the world in which I move, men and women speak freely to each other. Too freely, sometimes, perhaps."

"If I have offended you, pardon me," he repeated.

"Go on," she said, "I like to hear you speak."

It was his turn now to flush. The dark red blood mounted to his hair at this encomium.

"Yes, I view the ordinary marriage as a crime against your sex, Mrs. Marston. Man's vanity and wickedness have invented that possession attaches the woman while it detaches the man. It is a lie. I'll wager one hundred women to every man wrecks her delusions in the common life; but being more virtuous, more modest, than man, she clings wildly to the one to whom she has given all, and he, in his asinine brutishness and folly, mistakes a woman's despair for her love. Man has subjugated woman. He plumes himself on having won her."

Did his words arouse some far-away, faint echo in the young woman's breast? some vague remembrance or regret? some inner consciousness of the murder in herself of some quivering and exquisite thing? She shifted her seat uneasily, and withdrew more into the shadow so that he could not see her face.

"Yes," he continued, "when women protest, insist, that they are happy, they often make one think of children singing in the dark to prove they are not afraid of ghosts."

"Where is the balm?" she breathed rather than said.

"We have nothing to do with the remedies," he answered, with fatuity. "We destroy—pull down. Let the next generation rear up its temples on the ruins of the past. Sufficient unto us is to point the way, to clear away the débris, dig the foundations upon which they shall build. This is our work. Let them find theirs."

He threw back his hair with one hand, his attitude, his gesture, were full of exaltation. Fenno Asch lying in the hammock, her husband enjoying his placid cigar, reading his evening paper, flashed between them with an incongruity which almost moved her to laughter. She felt as if they—as if her husband—required some apology.

"There are men—good men—who only want to have the way shown to them. I assure you—I assure you—they are only waiting to be told what to do. You, yourself, if you had inherited capital, riches and power, would find it difficult—it is difficult! We . . . they want to do right."

"Do you think the ambulant fashion models who surround you—such a man, for instance, as I saw near you yesterday in the train—I do not know his name—has he one? —have distinct aspirations for relieving the race, have any knowledge of the injustice that broods at a stone's throw from their gloved hands? I ask for information. I am one of the . . . the people, the mass, an obscure, unknown identity, valueless, yet groping in darkness, suffering, with a brain to think, and I sometimes ask myself what such people imagine they were created for "

The impertinence of his speech almost staggered her, its shocking lack of taste. What right had he to cavil at her friends, to sound again that personal cry which she had purposely and tactfully avoided, to vex her with a question as difficult to answer as it was insolent to pose?

Yet if Percival Oakes desired to stand out before this woman, to force her to recognize that he was not the village schoolmaster as Opdyke was the doctor, and Mrs. Fesser postmistress, he had succeeded. Never again could she pass him by indifferently. She might despise or hate him, but he had sprung into an individuality, real, persistent, palpable. He had detached himself from the rest; but there was an impatience against him within her which must find vent.

"You must not judge people superficially, Mr. Oakes. I am surprised that you who look at all subjects so deeply should do so. The favored classes, as they are called, those who happen to have good clothes, and look to be amusing themselves, are often quite as unhappy as the rest. They cannot escape physical ills, nor treachery, calumny, ingratitude, which make us distrustful and cynical, and in injuring our characters inflict upon us irreparable harm. It is folly to imagine that the lack of money is the only misfortune. Only that which hurts what is best in us is of consequence. Can you, who are so intelligent, suppose that the poor have a monopoly of all the virtues, and that the rich, as they are called, lie forever on roses?"

She left her bench, and, reaching for her shoes, began to draw them on. She found the process difficult. They were hard and dry, having shrunk in the heat.

"I think the storm is passed. I must go."

"Will you permit me to help you?" he said, humbly.

"No, thanks. It is not necessary."

She adjusted her hat, and settled her light open jacket with a jerk.

"There, that will do. My veil is a ruin. I leave it on the table for the mice, with the remnant of our excellent meal."

"You will permit me to walk with you as far as your gate? I have no watch, but it must be nearly nine. It is quite dark."

"Yes, I have one. It is nine. Yes, certainly walk with me to the gate—see," she pushed open the door and stepped down into the grasses, "the storm is over, and the wind is so high it has nearly dried this sandy soil already." The moon was rising. It looked blood-red through the trees.

"I am glad it is drying," he said, with a short laugh. "I took refuge here not to wet my feet," and as she looked at him, surprised, "I did n't want to spoil my shoes," he said, simply. "They are the only decent ones I have; they are new. The old ones let in too much light."

She forgave him instantly, everything.

"I was very much interested in what you told me about your childhood, and your mother," she said, gently. "Some day perhaps I shall see you again, and you will tell me more."

She could not ask him to come and see her. She instinctively felt it would be unwise.

"I rarely speak of her. She was one of the unhappy ones—forsaken, embittered. Perhaps I draw from her some of my asperity. She used to talk very hardly of men. Poor women have not a high opinion of us. I am afraid you have thought me very . . . disagreeable. If you only knew, Mrs. Marston, how sorry I am to have perhaps annoyed you."

"No," she said, hurriedly. "I understand." Her lips trembled. She felt an uncontrollable desire to weep. They reached the gate. A star appeared on its other side, hanging midway between earth and heaven. It proved to be the end of Mr. Marston's cigar. This gentleman, in evening dress, with a wide-brimmed straw hat, loomed on the gravel. This hat was one of his affectations. He thought it had a country squire's negligence. It hung on a peg in the hall, and was invariably donned when very fastidious and conventional guests were expected.

To-day we will say to his credit it had been put on because it came nearest to his hand. He was beginning to be anxious. She gave her fingers lightly to Oakes for a moment, parting from him before her husband bridged the hundred yards that separated them.

"I was getting worried, dearest. Where were you during the storm? I sent the carriage around to Mrs. Taft's to see if you were still there. The dinner is waiting. It will be spoiled."

"I was there, but missed the carriage. I started before the worst, yet too late."

"Was that Taft with you?"

"No," she laughed. "Guess who?"

"Tommy Taft, then."

"No, Mr. Oakes, the young man that teaches the children." Her words seemed to settle him away again to a safe distance where such restless spirits, who could have no part among her household gods, should be kept. Nevertheless, although she had returned into Philistia, the curious desire to weep, which Oakes had awakened in her, remained. She felt as if upon her heart lay a leaden load of unshed tears.

"Where in the world did you pick him up?"

Somehow she resented the expression. She could not herself have explained why.

"He picked me up," she answered, quickly, "and was very nice to me indeed." She went on recounting her adventures.

"What could you find to say to him during a whole hour? He's a queer cuss, they tell me, a young fool. By the way, he's Mrs. Bush's beau."

"I can hardly believe that. He's so very superior to her," she said, coldly.

"Superior!"

"And he's not a fool. He has a beautiful face."

"A beautiful face! Are you joking, Lola? Oakes beautiful! Ha! ha! ha! That sallow, round-shouldered fellow! The lightning must have gotten into your eyes. Men do n't get much mashed on one another's good looks, but Asch, now I concede to you is a handsome man—*un beau mâle*, as the French have it. But Oakes, ah! ah!"

"Fenno looks like a figure in a coiffeur's window. Those long eyelashes of his are ridiculous."

"Has he a name?" the schoolmaster had asked her, and something in this query seemed to have lodged its echo in her breast. She remembered now with a certain shame how she had admired Asch's manly figure. How she had purred over him, and looked after his comforts as other women did, out of sheer imitation. Now, as she answered her husband with spirit, she could only remember Fenno's selfishness and the fact that she was getting just a little tired of him.

Oakes threaded his way through the underbrush, after Mrs. Marston left him, making a short cut back to the Dougherty house. The moon illumined it with its cool rays. The drops splashed from the eaves upon his head as he once more lifted the latch; they seemed a chrism of calm, a baptism of joy. He went in. The fire burned low. Its charred remains glowed lurid. He jabbed it with a fagot and threw on some cones. They sizzled for a moment, and then sent up a green flame. He seemed to see once more beside him that tender, graceful presence which had so long filled empty musings, lending beauty to their loneliness. By temperament he adored all feminine softness, was susceptible to sensuous charm. The hour spent with her in this dim hut, in these dank woods, seemed now unreal. Yet it was one of those chimeras which haunt the soul with divine ecstasy. He would have liked to ring its raptures to the skies. " Earth's bells do not chime in or toll our greatest joys or sorrows," he thought. She seemed to have left with him a certain peace. His angry protests against men and things were lulled, quenched for a moment by her influence. Perhaps she was right, he was unjust and superficial after all. He remembered how he had once detested a man whom he had known to be his enemy. He had vowed to do him hurt, but Providence took charge of his revenge, for the man became blind, and Oakes in the chances of life had met him and been compelled to cut his food for him. "How can one injure a blind man whose food one has to cut up," he thought, with a dry laugh. "Our enemies become blind and so disarm us." He remembered that the most dull-eyed youth he had known at school, apparently nerveless and obtuse, who studied not at all and ate enormously, had killed himself under peculiar, tragic circumstance because of a fancied stain upon his honor. What plenitude of profound experience could teach us to comprehend each other, to fathom motive, to solve character, to make allowance? Did the affectations of those whom he had called the "fashion models" necessarily betoken frivolity? Who could say? Perhaps they did hide something better. For her sake he was willing to believe it now.

Then he caught sight of her veil on the table, shriveled from the wetting it had got. He seized it, burying his face in its perfumed meshes. He opened his shirt and thrust it in. Rolling up his coat into a pillow, he stretched himself out before the fire. He would sleep here. Perhaps she would visit him again in dreams. And, as he lay there waiting, his fingers griped the bit of lace against his heart.

CHAPTER XVI

Mr. Marston was occupied. Archie Jr. had been ordered out of the house, where his noisy presence was intolerable. The servants trod softly. The dogs were chained at the stables lest their barking should disturb the master. Lola, in a white dressing gown, flitted anxiously from her apartment to his, when he nervously called her from the door of his open study. This study joined his bedroom. He had another downstairs next the *tabagie* which was dignified by the name of " office." The larger library fronting the terraces looked northward. From its shelves the valet Marvin had selected and brought up to his master numerous tomes. In these musty volumes Mr. Marston's nose had been buried a great part of the morning. They contained needed information as to American history and political development which had scourged his school days, but which he had long since forgotten. He was engaged in preparing his speech. The open-air meeting was to take place on the following Wednesday. It was now Monday. There was no time to waste. He called this preliminary travail "taking notes," but he knew that his only salvation lay in an elaborate composition, careful transcription to paper, with a final committal to memory. His memory was good. It had rarely played him pranks.

"How will this do, my dear?" he asked his wife for the eleventh time, as she timidly looked in, fearful of interfering with his industrious frenzy.

He began to read aloud to her a phrase of his peroration. It had seemed to him thoughtful and even elegant. Somehow, now that he listened to the sound of his own voice the words appeared flat and crude—the ideas *nil*.

"Of course," he explained, "sitting here in a loose coat with you, my love, it cannot be impressive as it will be delivered from a platform with the excitement of an audience upon me . . ."

There was no doubt of it. It sounded empty and withal pretentious.

"Don't you think, Archibald," she ventured, "that, in view of the simplicity of your hearers, it might be better to make it a little more . . . er . . . colloquial?"

"Colloquial?" Mr. Marston frowned.

"Yes, really it is too impressive, too finished. It reads to me a little like Racine."

"Racine!" Mr. Marston flushed, annoyed. You don't know my dear, what you are talking about. Racine—poppycock! . . . why, these are the very kind of people who demand some elaboration, some polish. Depend upon it, they appreciate style. My quarrel with our local orators is that they have a tendency to talk down to their audience instead of raising it to their own level. A grave mistake!"

He had never thought of this before, but it sounded well and would doubtless impress his wife, and he must defend his diction and dignity at any price.

"It may be so," said Lola, wagging her small head. "Read more that I may judge better." She closed her eyes, with the acute anguish which lay in their gentle depths, and prepared to listen. Her husband's whole career seemed at stake.

"Here, perhaps you will like this part. This about Abraham Lincoln, toward the end, 'the great, the just, the pure,' where is it? I've lost the page. The deuce take it! Ah, here it is."

"Yes, I like that. That is very well," said Lola, without enthusiasm.

"Those allusions to our great men always move a meeting of this kind to applause," said Mr. Marston. "I suppose a bit of that sort of buncombe is expected."

"Yes, of course," said Lola.

"Well?"

"When you make the speech, dear, do you speak so very, very fast? I should think the people in the back seats would have difficulty in following."

"I know you are right. I do get racing. I must correct this one serious fault. I thank you for your valuable suggestion, my dear. I will stand up now behind the table and try to get up the right speed. One must not be ponderous."

Racine rankled, but he made an effort to be patient. She was a clever woman, and if one wishes to learn one must be receptive and supple—not mulish. He placed one hand upon the table, the other lightly in the flap of his smoking-jacket where his heart was supposed to perform its pumping processes. He began again to deliver his speech. His slow enunciation of each syllable, heavy, colorless, without inflection, filled her with dismay. She found she could not follow the subject, so drowsy did her senses grow in the monotony of his tones.

"I think you might, perhaps, speak a wee bit more rapidly than that."

He glared. "Don't you comprehend— I'm only practicing to cure myself of overmuch speed. Really, Lola, you might help me instead of saying discouraging things to me."

"You tell me you have spoken at dinners. How did you get on then, dear?"

"I'm not an orator. I know it. I have only got on my legs two or three times in my life. I cut it very short. I got through. I was among friends."

"It must be just too awful not to . . . get through," said Mrs. Marston.

"Nonsense, I don't mean to make a fiasco on Wednesday. A delegation is coming over from Flushing; you may depend upon it I shall not make an ass of myself if I can help it."

Mrs. Marston said she felt confident that he would not.

"Fancy," she said, reflectively, "your making an ass of yourself!" Then, after a pause: "Suppose you suddenly forgot the speech when you had learned it!" A new terror thrilled her.

"I shall take my notes along."

"Ah!"

"If the worst comes to the worst I can read from them."

"I don't think that would be nice at all." She shook her head again decidedly.

"I don't know about it's not being nice, my dear, but such things have been done. You seem to be a regular alarmist to-day. I declare you quite make me nervous. I expect to throw the thing off without a moment's hesitancy. I have a very fair memory. I think when one has this gift it is better not to speak impromptu. One may make a show of one's self and spoil everything."

She agreed with him that it would indeed be dreadful to make a show of one's self.

Turning over the pages of his manuscript he found a tit-bit, something local and humorous, at which he laughed himself, a hit of which he was immensely proud, and which he read to her.

"That'll fetch them!"

His wife, however, to his chagrin, did not laugh at all. She looked quite careworn, almost haggard. It was evident she had missed his point.

"Don't you think that funny?"

"Well, yes, it is rather funny," she said, after a moment's hesitancy.

The announcement of the twelve o'clock

breakfast brought the seance to a temporary conclusion.

When the day came, the Marston family—Mr. Marston in a long frock coat with a carnation in his button-hole, Lola ethereal in gray mull, little Archie in duck trousers and a sailor collar—got into the phaeton. Fenno Asch drove May Plunkett in a Tilbury, Mrs. Ayrault and de Beaumont came bumping behind in a village cart. They thought it an enormous frolic. Mrs. Marston had explained to the Count the necessity of gentlemen in the United States interesting themselves in politics, of establishing terms of friendliness and sympathy with their country neighbors, and of playing the *gentilhomme campagnard* with urbanity and tact. The Count screwed in his monocle, waved one arm in the ether, and said he "seized the situation." It was just the same in France, at St. Quentin, near which was his mother's estate. He often addressed the people from the balcony, and then invited them in to supper, since the Republic had leveled all classes. One must march with the times, make concessions. One's heart might be with the king, but reason must be with the nation. He told his mother this, but it was difficult. She was a little *arriérée*. She was a Rohan, an obstinate royalist. He himself felt that he had a sacred duty to perform to the Republic. Mrs. Ayrault, who had heard all this before, gave a little grin behind her fan.

"The bird that flew out of the ark was about as liberal as you are," she said, while she briskly tucked in her shapely limbs, and the Count's lank ones under the light lap-robe. " Don't talk rot."

"You are *ravissante*," said the Count, leaning back in rapture.

May Plunkett, skillfully driven by her handsome escort, was very silent. She had a problem to solve. Should she marry Fenno Asch, who had never offered himself to her, and never meant to. So many had!— Or should she wed the St. Louis Colonel? The latter had offered. Of this there could be no shadow of doubt. He had offered himself and many other things. She was weighing the pros and cons. Womanlike, she began with the cons. As she laid them down she qualified them:

CONS.

Over fifty—not much consequence.

Widower—no consequence.

Two daughters—married, therefore out of the way.

Has attacks of gout—pretty bad.

Gets red in the face and blusters—unpleasant.

Not well-born—unfortunate.

Purse-proud—regrettable.

Says gauche and stupid things—horrible.

No appreciation of art or literature, little education—might be improved.

PROS.

Good-looking, manly—cheering attributes.

Twenty millions—a mere figure to a girl accustomed to luxury, but, her money being yet in anticipation, comfortable.

Two palaces already built, will build any number more, anywhere, at a moment's notice; fine horses, coaches, yachts already—amusing.

Not dissipated—a good thing always, of course.

Very much in love with her—was this a pro or a con?—she was inclined to think the latter, as, so far, she found his love extremely disagreeable.

Had distinguished himself in the war—picturesque.

When they reached the grounds she was just summing up her charges to the jury, her friends.

In spite of the democratic tendencies of

the day, front seats had been reserved for the Marston party. Percival Oakes, who was one of the ushers, took off his hat gravely to Mrs. Marston, and conducted her to her place. The misty folds of her gown brushed him as she nodded and spoke a word. She installed herself between Archie Jr., who had his papa's overcoat on his arm (Mr. Marston was to accompany the delegation back to Flushing, where a reception was to be held—he might not get home until late), and Fenno Asch. Percival Oakes, as he designated the seats to the ladies, looked at him.

The day was brilliant. Over their heads floated a snow-white cloud, shaped like a shield. It might have been the sacred Ancile, fixed there triumphant to guard them from all ills. The rest of heaven was of a vivid blue, burnished, blinding. Lola, blinking, raised her gray parasol. Behind her sat Joe Bush, Beth and Dottie. Beth, resplendent in a new foulard, brave with its grape-vine pattern; Dottie, starched in a fresh print, the gold locket and chain fastened about her little throat. Beth followed Mrs. Marston's example, and raised her sunshade—the one of which she was so proud. She noticed that her mistress's had no lace upon it. Her eyes fastened themselves upon every detail of Mrs. Marston's, Mrs. Ayrault's, and Miss Plunkett's toilettes. If their hats were in the latest fashion then had her Third Avenue milliner basely deceived and cheated her. The brims were narrower than hers. The woman's perfidy filled Beth's soul. The sun was darkened to her. She noticed with wonder that the tiny locks in Miss Plunkett's neck were out of curl and lay limp upon a chiffon fichu which was a trifle rumpled, while the sequins upon Mrs. Ayrault's yellow bodice were somewhat tarnished; yet the effect the three women produced among the crowd of gaping villagers was startling. They distanced everybody by the mere way they held their heads and hands, spoke to each other in that mutual *camaraderie* with its masonry of cabalistic signals so easy to strive for, so hard to acquire.

Next to the Bush family sat the Pullens. Floribel, charming in her simple cloth frock with its scarlet necktie, and Mrs. Pullen in black bombazine, crisp crape veil, and neat black gloves. Why she should thus appear always in deep mourning, was one of the unanswered questions of the neighborhood, for her husband had died thirty years before, and her son was living. On official occasions Floribel always decked her mother in this careful livery of woe. She was a gaunt, toothless crone, with a high-bumped forehead and hatchet cheeks, but so dressed she looked quite lady-like and imposing. Probably Floribel thought that when a woman has passed the age of love-making such habiliments are suitable and safe.

Pierre Rose, who had come across the meadows with some of the maids to hear the master speak, stared fixedly at Miss Pullen. She did not return his amorous oglings, but they did not appear to inspire her with resentment. All the annoyance they invoked was plainly painted upon the features of the gentleman who was wedged between her and Dottie Bush. One of the neighbors had once called him the "black-browed beetle." The description suited him passably. He was insectivorous in size and color, and looked distinctly mischievous.

"If you're flirting with that Frenchman, Florrie, it's time I quit," he whispered in her ear.

"What Frenchman, Mr. Pear?" said Florrie, sweetly, the embodiment of unjustly accused virginity.

"I ain't as blind as I may look," went on the lover; "if there's more than one Frenchman in this assembly I guess I'd know it."

"Well, there is then more than one

Frenchman, so there! I declare I believe you're jealous," she said, shrugging her shoulders and smiling.

"Jealous? Jealous of a cook? When I've sunk as low as that, Miss Pullen, I'll seek another friend. . . ."

"Well now, Mr. Pear, you are mistaken for once. There is more than one Frenchman here. That gentleman in front with Mrs. Marston is a French gentleman, and he's a Count, too!"

"You'll be making eyes at him next, Florrie. I guess it would just about suit your fancy to be a Countess."

"I wouldn't marry a Papist not for any title," said Miss Pullen, tossing her head.

"You'd have to go to confession and tell all your sins. That wouldn't suit you, eh?" He bent his head forward eager to catch her answer.

"That is against Bible injunction according to me," said Florrie. "You oughtn't to tell your secrets. The Scripture says 'and thy left hand shall not know what thy right hand doeth.' Isn't that right, ma?"

Mrs. Pullen nodded her head with a feeble gurgle of approbation.

"Yes, daughter, that's so," she said.

"Well, you're a clever minx, anyway," said Mr. Pear, somewhat mollified by this peculiar interpretation of gospel truth. There's no catching you, is there—eh, Florrie?"

But the Count was not glancing toward Floribel; he was seeking, as ever, the sorcery which lay for him in Arden Ayrault's velvet eyes.

By-and-by Floribel's city lover, seeing Rose's maneuvers to attract her attention, came back to the attack.

"I don't care if it's a French Count or cook, or that athlete out of the circus you were talking with. Yes, I caught you, last spring. I won't stand it. If you carry on, I'll quit," he repeated, with an angry scowl at Pierre.

"Pshaw! That athlete! Why, I was just showing him our view over the fence. A nice young man. You call that talking, Mr. Pear?" She stifled a yawn. "I declare I'm getting sleepy."

The jealousy of the man one loves is delicious, of the man one tolerates, fatiguing. Miss Pullen liked pretty presents, but she liked agreeable words even better. She was pleasure-loving. She was getting very tired of her adorer. She thought with contempt that he was willing to hurt, and yet afraid to strike.

The brass band tuned its instruments, and

broke into an overture. A beneficent interlude. Mrs. Marston turned and spoke to the Bushes.

"I have n't seen you for a long time, Mrs. Bush."

"You don't come up much to the cottage, Mrs. Marston." Her voice had a reproach in it which never failed to arouse latent antagonism in Lola's breast.

"I will come in a day or two. I 've been engaged with guests and other things." Lola was determined to be gracious.

"I have got some new pullets to show you, Mrs. Marston." She would not say ma'am, as she would have said to Mrs. Opdyke; she feared it might be servile. She went on: "And Wilhelmina has a heifer, dropped last night."

Lola shook hands with Floribel, whom she liked. She also addressed the girl's mother. "How are you, Mrs. Pullen?"

"Well, ma'am, I 've got the plumbago and the bronkity so my tubes is some paralyzed, but I 'm pretty fair, I thank you."

She did not care for the stories against the girl. She thought they were probably mere gossip. Her manners were certainly modest, and she was always dressed so neatly.

"You look splendid, Mrs. Marston. Just

splendid. So fat and beautiful. You are not the fat kind, but you look real plump for you. And Master Archie! Isn't he too cute for anything! How are you, sir? Shake hands. You haven't forgotten Pepper, have you? Come in and see him some day. Ma's taught him some new tricks."

Archie gave Miss Pullen his hand politely, and asked some questions about her terrier, which he had sometimes stopped to frolic with.

Floribel spoke of Marston Terrace and its loveliness. "I was over the other day," she said. "We are so proud to have the place here so near us. It's a regular show place for all our visitors. We are proud of having you for a neighbor."

Beth, whose secret admiration for Mrs. Marston was far more profound and complex, marveled at Floribel's easy exposition of her sentiments.

Floribel's blood was not curdled. It was a healthy fluid, from which the processes of circulation eliminated acids. It assimilated neither envy nor malice.

"Yes, now do come and see Pepper, little dear!" Mrs. Pullen was saying to Archie, in her husky whisper. She was one of those well-trained American mothers who invariably follow their daughters' initiative. She had never been known since Floribel's birth to disagree with her or to speak first.

"I was going away this week," continued Floribel, "but I wouldn't miss Mr. Marston's speech, no, not for anything. We all came to hear him. I told my friend in Atlantic City she'd have to wait."

Lola explained that her husband was not an orator, and had only come to please his party, at which Floribel shook her head incredulously. She was sure Mr. Marston must be a grand speaker.

With a sudden bray the band stopped. A hush fell. The first speaker was introduced. He was a man rough in dress, unshaven, awkward, ungrammatical, yet somehow he held attention. The child in the second row forgot to fret, the old soldier who took the tickets, to cough and spit, the belated schoolgirls crouching on the platform steps, to titter. He was plausible, lucid, intelligible, above all fluent. Fluency is a moral not an intellectual attribute. The higher flights of eloquence spring more from character than from culture. Calm, composed, master of his audience, and of himself, he seemed to enjoy his own power. He sat down after fifteen minutes, which had seemed but five, amid clapping of hands and some shouts of "Good, good!"

Another speaker followed, more pretentious, better dressed, in black broadcloth, with a white cravat; a state legislator. He had the paunch and profile of a papal prelate with an unctiousness which he had in fact acquired while a student in a college dominated by the Order of Jesus. He, too, was a success. Easy, urbane, by turns earnest or satirical, he possessed imagination and dramatic quality. He held his hearers. He retired amid a burst of cheers. It was then that Mr. Marston got upon his feet.

He began. Lola noticed that his skin was of a greenish hue, his lips parched, his eyes restless and vacant. His hair seemed to have arisen about his head like a halo of rays; perhaps it was the heat. It looked singular. She made a sign to him with her hand to smooth it down. He did not seem to understand her, and stopped short in his speech, looking about helplessly. There was a pause. He cleared his throat and began again. He went on fairly well for five minutes more or less. The Bible's thousand years came to Lola's mind. What was time? A mere unit of misery. Twisting on her hard plank, she felt it so. Then—then—there came a pause indeed—a pause long, awful, blood-curdling. From green his complexion seemed to become leaden—livid.

His eyes glazed in their sockets. The old soldier hawked and snorted. The girls giggled and choked. The baby began to scream. Mr. Marston looked toward them all in turns and smiled—such a smile! Lola had never seen it on any other human being's countenance, much less on that of the husband whom she loved. It might be that of a lost spirit just consigned to eternal doom. He was feeling for his notes! In his coat, his vest, his trousers, everywhere, anywhere! His notes! The worst had befallen him, the horrible contingency. His mind was a blank. The speech had vanished, but alas! not only from his memory, but from his pockets! They were empty! The cursed, cursed things met him with vacuum. He gasped, "Overcoat!"

It was then that Oakes rose to the occasion; in pity for the woman he revered, he sprang to the assistance of the man he despised. He understood. In an instant he had grasped the overcoat from Archie's trembling fingers, wrested the notes from their hiding-place, and handed them to Mr. Marston. It is positive that there are times when we could kiss the garments of those whose lack of humor at other moments irritates. With gratitude ineffable Lola realized that Oakes had seized the tragedy of the situation, not its absurdity. His jaws might have been made of iron, his forehead of steel; not a line, not a vestige of ridicule traversed the mask of his imperturbable seriousness. He had saved her husband. His action imposed upon the audience. The glance with which she rewarded him was one full of such poignant sweetness that he almost died, inundated with the happiness it brought to him.

Marvin, the idiot, had put the papers in the overcoat instead of in the vest as directed. Mr. Marston had time to feel that dismissal would be too good for his valet, that death by torture could hardly atone. He wished the crafty Torquemada was still living to invent a new mode of lingering execution. Fumbling, faint, he fingered the pages,—faint but rescued!

What did it matter that the people were beginning to chatter, to scrape their feet, that a voice, quickly quelled but plainly audible, cried out, " He ain't no good. Marston ain't no good"? Let his enemies do their worst—he had . . . the notes!

He went on, faster, and faster, and faster, showering the platitudes he had strung together until they seemed to Lola a mere medley of incoherent words. He skipped the witty sally. He was in no mood for joking. With the final invocation to Lincoln, which he delivered so inaudibly that it missed its mark, he sat down, while the band played "Hail to the Chief." There was a round of brief but palpably forced applause. There was more speaking and more music. To Lola all was over. The sting of her husband's failure brought cold drops of moisture to her brow, and she shivered, though not with cold. To see the nullity of one we respect, even in so slight a test, is a form of suffering Dante omitted from his purgatorial cleansings. Children who first discover the faults of parents, their makeshifts, or incompetence, are in this sad plight. The Count, however, was profuse in his commendations of Mr. Marston's speech. It is true he had not heard a word of it, but with his native gallantry and kindness he saw his hostess was uncomfortable, and came to her rescue with such amends as he could make. He even told her that her husband was a second Mirabeau.

"Look here," Mrs. Ayrault whispered to him, "don't make a donkey of yourself. It was horrible, and she knows it. Poor dear! For God's sake, let her alone."

Fenno Asch had been so bored that a pall of deep dejection enveloped him.

Why in the devil's name should Marston desire to do such things? Why men should choose to assume these absurd responsibilities he could not for the life of him imagine. Ten minutes of that nasty, ill-smelling crowd had been quite enough for him. Even Miss Plunkett's taut figure, as the young lady sprang to her place by his side, was refracted upon a jaundiced retina. She represented an unwholesome nuptial temptation, which he attributed to the bourgeois atmosphere just inhaled. He was so rude to her on the way home that the St. Louis Colonel's boom again fluctuated upward. May told herself that if the Colonel was rough with others he was always a lamb with her. She decided that Fenno was a brute. The valiant Colonel's chances received an impetus which bowled hopefully with every revolution of the Tilbury's wheel. A man is less repulsive when he has declared himself.

Oakes, plodding home through the fields, could not enjoy the discomfiture of him whom he so cordially disliked. Its cost had been too great. He had seen what *she* endured. It was the blind man over again. The impotence, the sarcasm of fate which pursued all his hates. But she had leaned to him in gratitude, and he had served her! This seemed enough!

A few days later the schoolmaster left Paradise. He went into the great city with his small wardrobe and his box of books. He went and was swallowed up. Its dark waves closed over him, leaving no sign.

CHAPTER XVII

Beth had bowed to Percival Oakes across the knot of Mrs. Marston's pale brown hair, with a smile in which there lurked an invitation. His inscrutable regard crossed hers coldly like the glint from some steel weapon. He returned her salutation, but gave no heed to its summons.

Her anger had cooled. She missed him. She was not of a caliber calculated to captivate her neighbors. They had viewed her arrival with that measure of interest which narrow communities evince toward strangers. Too self-engrossed to be sympathetic, her value to them had soon been gauged. She took but scant interest in their affairs, and her longing to be above them, even in its meager achievement, was, while not fully understood, yet obscurely guessed.

"She's awful proud," somebody had said of her.

"She's that stuck up she thinks herself bigger 'n Mrs. Marston, and puts on a sight more airs."

"Mrs. Marston don't put on airs. She's a real lady, but Miss Bush, she seems afeard people will trespass on her."

So ran the village tattle.

Yes, she missed him. She had in vain waited for a call—a note—some sign—none came. Then, biting her lips with vexation, she had herself written a short, friendly line—not an apology—asking him to tea. He declined with an excuse which was evidently an invention, that false change which deceives nobody. Then it was that she fully realized all she had lost. Even his egotism had found a niche in her life. Few in their wish to please but are base enough to pander to the egotist, and talk to him about himself. Beth proved no exception; but Oakes's egotism was of a kind which charmed her without wearying. So she at least had some excuse. His advanced views and militant humor had become like wine to her, a form of dissipation resembling the violent pleasures of alcohol. She could not forego it without pain. The dull pain of a dull existence, which felt that above it, just above it, so near that she could touch it with her hand, lay another life, mysterious, dazzling, which through some trick of a lost birthright passed her by. It was the sights and sounds from the great house which kept her dissatisfied and unhappy. She sometimes wished it and its occupants could be shut out of her ken forever, wished it with a persistence growing to mania. Lack of air and exercise, too frequent libations of strong tea, absence of all mental occupations, aggravated these unhealthy broodings. Since Oakes came no more she rarely went out; she had no love of nature, and long walks always fatigued her more than her household work. She missed the mental friction of his visits. Then she learned that he had left Paradise.

Upon her lay the full weight of her sacrifice. She determined to cease complaining, to be a good wife, a good mother, to close her ears to the solicitations of folly, to be a happy and helpful woman. Somehow the endeavor, praiseworthy in itself, was a trifle ponderous, lacked lightness. Elizabeth, in fact, was not elastic.

Joe, after the manner of husbands, seemed not to remark the change in her, or, if he did, scarcely to be grateful. He had often been fain to escape from her tongue. He found himself now somewhat oppressed by her silences. There are silences harder to bear than words. Their sting lies in the fact that they must be ignored, whereas open reproach may be met with scorn. But Elizabeth was doing her best. In moments of impatience she now held her peace. She went about her work as the animals do, with a sort of blind obedience to rule. In the lairs of caves and of woods, in the depths of seas, in the nests of singing birds, in the holes of insects, there is ever going on this watchful wakefulness, this sleepless industry, this devotional renouncement. The beasts teach us something better than their brutal instincts of pleasure, other things besides the uses of their self-love and craftiness. They preach to us law and order. The universe is a great reformatory. In it the inexorable doctrines of self-sacrifice are taught. Through all the torment of desire, through all the raging wish to grow, to widen, and to shine, an iron hand bears down, and the preservation of the species is insured. Secret of secrets at which mute man looks up, marveling and frightened. Deep down within Beth's heart there lay that cryptic wonder, that occult "why?" If Oakes had not forsaken her, if she could have rallied from a desertion which she attributed to his profound contempt, her task would have seemed easier. His friendship, much as he was disliked in Paradise, had cast a prestige over her, for if he was disliked he was admired. She had reveled in his society, proud to have him seen beside her, liking to have the people know he was her friend. How she envied Floribel, the *insouciance*, which made her seem as happy in the fellowship of that scaramouch, that whining ferret, her dark lover, as in that of a capricious and yellow-haired young poet. Floribel possessed the temperament which is uninfluenced by surrounding, which creates its own atmosphere. Beth's laboratory knew no such alchemy. She belonged to that sisterhood dependent on environment. A word could plunge her into heaven or scourge her to the pit. When such is the soil, the seed a passing bird shall drop roots quickly in the harrowed track.

Lola reproached herself for her late lack of concern about the weal of her whilom barnyard pets, her apathy at the birth of Wilhelmina's heifer, her supineness as to dairy visiting. It was a long time since she had watched the maids churning and forming the melting gold. In Mrs. Daggett's day she had found leisure for all this. We always have the leisure to follow inclination. She told herself that it was all because of her farmer's wife, of the dislike which she felt for her. She disliked to be in the room with her, even to catch sight of her in the distance, and she chafed at herself for being so unreasonable. Mrs. Bush was not worth such animosity.

"Dear me," she said to Mrs. Ayrault one morning, "I suppose I must pull myself up to the cottage, and take some interest in things generally. The butter was poor last week."

The little party, disbanded after Mr. Marston's political eclipse, had now returned to pass the Sunday which was the last of summer. May Plunkett had driven over with some young people to play tennis. It was warm, and she and Asch left the others and came to ask for lemonade.

"It will be fun," said Arden.

"Fun?" I don't like the woman. I don't think I can stand her much longer. She is so pretentious, so queer, and I don't understand her. She embarrasses me. There is no fun in scolding her, as I must, about the butter. She will probably be insolent. I am always expecting it from her."

Mrs. Ayrault sighed.

"Why do you sigh, dearest?"

"I sigh because I have missed my vocation."

"Your vocation?"

"Yes. I was just made for this; to look after butter and eggs and chickens, and farmers' wives, and quarrel with them about the cream; to have babies, to fondle and sew for them, to see that their pantalets were properly embroidered as our great grandmothers used. I was created for domestic joys. I am a dog-woman playing the cat. A dog-woman with a big, faithful dog's heart, who is playing at being a syren, and who makes a jolly mess of it.

"This is a new light upon you," said Lola, laughing.

"No, it is not; but you're so innocent, and so sweet, just as sweet as sugar candy! Anybody can impose upon you. I have. I have also imposed on Beaumont. On you because you are so ingenuous, on him because he is so perverted. He thinks me vain, wayward, capricious, untractable, possibly false—everything a man of his type most adores. I, in fact, have no vanity, no caprice, am not wayward enough to turn that silly weather-cock over there spinning on your lawn, and as to falseness—bah! the very thought of it makes me sick. I loathe it. I am truth embodied. Pretense and sham bore me so that they give me a pain in my face, throat, and ears. Yes, really, when I try to flatter, for instance, just a little, just to keep my hand in, I have to send for the doctor and take pills. I was made for a *pot au feu* existence, with my gude man opposite smoking his pipe, my bairnes frolicking at my knee, while I re-heeled the family stockings, or read 'Pilgrim's Progress' aloud. And now this being so, let us go up and examine the lurid Mrs. Bush, who no doubt will look upon me with disapprobation as upon a dangerous, wicked enchantress, when I know perfectly well I'm a decent, respectable, reasonable person, with no more evil in me than a common house-fly, and about as much fascination as a drone bumble-bee."

Some stragglers came in just in time for Mrs. Ayrault's climax. It was received with laughter, and a general clamor ensued to be allowed to witness the impression Mrs. Ayrault would produce on the "lurid Bush."

The lemonade having been sipped, May Plunkett and Asch, Mrs. Ayrault and Lola, the Count, and one or two others picked up their respective hats, parasols, and walking sticks, and were soon ascending the path that lead up to the cottage. It ran between deciduous bushes, up a gentle declivity, until it emerged upon the open ground which environed the farm buildings.

On that very morning another unpleasant little scene had occurred between Bush and his master. Two of the farm hands got drunk. Their work was neglected. Mr.

Marston, vexed, rebuked Joe for inefficiency in controlling the men under him.

"You do your own work well enough," he said, "but you don't seem to have any faculty for making others work, or controling them. They are not afraid of you, therefore your orders are ineffectual."

Now Joe knew this—Mr. Marston had put his finger in a wound. He winced. We rarely acknowledge the weakness in ourselves which we know to be paramount. Joe became somewhat dogged.

"I tries to please ye," he kept repeating in his usual refrain, dull-eyed, exasperating.

"It's no question of pleasing. I say it's unfortunate, most unfortunate, when the foreman can't get work and obedience out of his men. They get drunk three days out of the week, and you have to look to all their duties as well as your own."

"I ain't lazy," said Joe, deprecatingly.

"Who says you're lazy? Do I? Nobody charges you with laziness. What I say is that you have no faculty as an overseer, and on this place that is what I want."

Then Joe became a trifle testy, and said if men had the devil of drink in them he didn't see what he was to do about it. All he could promise was to keep sober himself, which being logical was provoking. Mr.

Marston rebuked him sharply for his reply, and they parted not the best of friends. There was again that vague threat of dismissal which filled Joe with despair, because he liked his place, prized its advantages, and was by nature averse to change. He knew that he could find nothing that he liked better, and looked back with a certain terror upon the unremunerative responsibilities of his mother's farm. To gauge our own limitations and to love those who point them out to us, is not the same process. By an impulse extremely unusual to him, he threw down his rake and came up to find his wife. His heart was sore within him. He half hoped she would receive his outpoured plaint—for he told her what had passed, dwelling on his wrongs—with fire as of old. He felt that it would relieve his sense of injustice done, since he himself had no gift of expression, and his own indignation had always more of an element of sorrow in it than of anger.

But, true to her resolves, Beth, dry-lipped, dry-eyed, listened but answered not. Thoroughly a woman, living more in one present minute than in decades of the future, the thought of possible dismissal nevertheless made her sick and faint. And for incompetence!—her husband's! hers! What a triumph for the servants over there! For the men and maids she had offended—for Pierre Rose, whom she knew to be her unforgiving enemy. What a stain before the villagers to whom these nearer ones would soon betray the truth with covert jeers. Not that!—not that! They would themselves give warning, throw up the place, but never —never—never acknowledge that they were beaten and undone in such a way as this.

If I seem to exaggerate so trifling an incident as a threatened change of farmers by a Long Island landowner, I have failed to portray Beth as she was. What makes us smile, we who mayhap have wider horizons and larger hopes, to her was terrible and tragical. So she gulped down her passion of resentment, and spoke quite firmly and wisely—to Joe's infinite amazement—actually advising a stronger hand over the men, and pacific measures with "the Marstons." She spoke of them thus with an infinite contempt of intonation, but with no outward sign of violence or ill-will.

He returned to his work and she to her reflections, but neither had gone far before the sound of voices and of steps upon the gravel flurried Beth to the conclusion that visitors were approaching.

Picking their way through the shrubbery,

passing the "Colony," a white pavilion between the house and farm where an overflow of bachelor guests sometimes found shelter, Mrs. Marston and her friends had reached the cottage porch. Now all women should know better than to invade the farmer's wife's domains at half-past eleven of a morning, when she is sure to be among her pots and kettles, her washing, baking, brewing, or dinner-getting, and Beth, even though she kept a "slavey," and wore lace on her parasol, was no exception to the rule.

She was a trifle unkempt, a bit bedraggled. She had just time to beat a hasty retreat, to scuffle quickly up to her bedroom, from where she called to "Jane" for a moment's parley.

Jane, red-handed, mealy from her breadmaking, appeared upon the stairs.

"It's Miss Marston and the folks from the big house," she announced in a stage whisper, with witless gestures and silly noddings.

"Ask them into the best parlor, tell 'em I'll be down in half a second, and here—stop, Jane,"—Beth grew agonized, for Jane had already disappeared. She had heard, however, and came back.

"I'm here, Miss Bush."

"Throw open one of the shutters, only

one, do you hear, and just pass a duster over the table. I ain't been in there to-day to do my dusting."

With more cabalistic signs and posturings, Jane once more vanished.

Beth heard her open the door. A light step crossed the threshold. There was a rattling at the shutter beneath. The girl was obeying her commands.

A sense of discouragement invaded Beth when she caught sight of her soiled calico, her hair done up in its matutinal curl papers, her finger-nails, and her complexion. There was no time to be lost. Galvanized into febrile action by the sounds below—they told her that only Mrs. Marston had entered the cottage and that the others were conversing with her from the porch through the open window—Beth tore the papers from her forehead, hastily tossed up her hair, wiped off her face and hands on a damp towel, disengaged herself at a bound from her skirt and bodice. For an instant she stood irresolute. What should she put on? From below she could hear the conversation. Her name was mentioned. She paused intent to listen. Were they laughing at her already? But the words were innocent.

"Mrs. Bush is very fortunate to have

such a pretty little house. I could live here myself, with the man of my heart," Miss Plunkett was saying.

"Your . . . er . . . what?" asked Fenno Asch.

"O, you need n't sneer, Mr. Asch. I 'm serious. I say I could give up worldly ambitions for . . ."

"Don't talk twaddle, May," said Mrs. Ayrault. "Mr. Asch's interrogation is legitimate and even well-timed. You need n't pout and toss your mane. We 've heard of the Colonel, and the dance you 're leading him."

"You see the Colonel does n't exactly offer love in a cottage," said May, laughing.

"Poor thing! Is it his fault that everything he looks at turns to gold?"

"Even mademoiselle's hair," said de Beaumont.

"If you mean by that, Monsieur de Beaumont, that my hair is n't a natural product . . . or that the Colonel dares . . ."

"*Dieu m'en garde Mademoiselle*, I said . . ."

"If we had found a nice old-fashioned farmhouse on this place," Lola was explaining from her place at the window-sill, "I doubt if Mr. Marston ever would have built. We could have added and tinkered, and been romantic and uncomfortable, but now

I am glad he built, for the house is the apple of his eye."

"Your house is charming," said Mrs. Ayrault. "So airy, and wide, and cool. And I think you like it too."

"O, I adore my home," said Lola. Her words, mellifluously spoken, came direct to Elizabeth's straining ears.

In the meantime the dice was cast. Some evil genius surely held the cup. From a dark corner of her closet Beth detached the tea-gown. It looked strangely pink on this bright morning. Her fingers grew awkward amid its intricacies. Clumsily pulling at buttons, seeking for strings, fluffing up bows of ribbon, she put it on. She did so waveringly, with hesitation and doubt. When she approached the mirror she thought herself hideous. Should she tear the thing off and cast it from her as being a demoniacal temptation, don the crisp calico which lay at hand, fresh from the iron, suitable and trim? But the desire to appear at leisure, elegant, a lady, in the eyes of these people carried the day. The tradition of the Mascotte holds a grain of verisimilitude. If we have not all mascottes we are at least prone to believe in the power of their opposites. Certain persons seem to bring us trouble. It is positive that there are those who always find us at a disadvantage. Their visits appear timed to meet our ruffled tempers, our disturbed digestions, our disarranged coiffures, and this invariably, persistently, through years of vain effort to snap and conquer the fateful spell they weave. Are they never to find us calm, dignified and dressed, at rest with them and the world? Their announcement at last seems a portent of disaster, their heralding a menace, their very name a hidden threat, their presence a calamity. Is it possible that upon so feeble a web as a pink garment, poor Beth had hung her future and its peace?

Pinning a recalcitrant fold about her throat, tripping over the front breadth, which was an inch too long, thrusting an escaped hairpin in her hair, with a heart beating to bursting and a hand shaking with agitation, Beth crossed the hall. Mrs. Marston had never seen the tea-gown. Beth knew it. It was for this she had put it on. She thought it such a pity that it should waste and fade, and Mrs. Marston never know! If its investiture produced surprise, on Mrs. Marston's face there was no sign. She drew her chair a little from the window in her light gracious way, greeting Mrs. Bush in her low voice, half drowned by the gayety from the porch, which, it must be confessed, was waxing boisterous.

"Your friends are merry," said Beth, with a pinched smile. "Would they like to come in?"

"No, I think not. I only ran up for a moment just to ask about Wilhelmina, and to speak about the butter. They are waiting for me."

Then Beth, ill at ease, beating about for a topic, launched as usual into those complaints which never failed to arouse Lola's ire.

"The dairy's damp," she said. "I ain't been used to one under ground. It's no wonder the butter gets a taste. Now down in Pontifex . . ."

"We give everything that's required," said Lola, not quite gently.

Beth saw her annoyance, and the demands of hospitality forced her to hold out the olive branch.

Would Mrs. Marston have a glass of cherry wine she had made herself? She asked it with the majesty of an empress, and called "Jane" in the tone with which Cleopatra might have summoned Charmian. Lola, willing to be mollified, assented. She did not like such cordials, but when Jane brought it, after a very long delay, she tasted it good-naturedly and handed glasses through the window to her guests, and chatted pleasantly. By-and-by the conversation flagged so hopelessly that she got up to leave. Beth accompanied her to the door. Their apparition produced a curious hush. All eyes were turned.

"It's Mrs. Bush," said Lola, addressing the company in general and no one in particular, with a slight movement of the hand.

Asch got up, stretched himself, and yawned. de Beaumont brought his heels together with a click, and bowed low, taking off his straw hat with its blue ribbon. May Plunkett said:

"Oh, Mrs. Bush, I think your cottage is such a dear."

Mrs. Ayrault adjusted her lorgnon. Beth shivered as it swept her figure into its comprehensive focus.

"How are you, Mrs. Bush?" she said, with a slightly sarcastic inflection and illy concealed amusement. I hope we have n't disturbed you. We're a noisy lot, I'm afraid. Mrs. Marston wanted to leave us at home, but we insisted upon coming up to see you, and we're so *glad* now that we did. Your cherry wine is excellent—thanks!" As she spoke she handed her half-emptied glass to Beth, whose fingers had been outstretched for a handshake, and who received it sidewise, dripping its lees upon the trimmings of her strange raiment. She sought some word which came not, with which to quench this handsome, mocking woman. With those quick instincts which lie inherent in American women Beth had divined the effect that she produced. She saw herself . . . ridiculous. Yes, and when a few moments later their words, their jests, came back to her, she knew.

"Did you ever see such a guy?" said Fenno Asch.

"Does she always get herself up so?" said May Plunkett, "or was it for our special benefit?"

"In my country," said de Beaumont, "the *maîtresses fermières* wear a blue cotton apron and cap."

"Mrs. Bush," said Arden, "was certainly wonderful."

Et tu, Brute! For above all pierced Lola's verdict. "She was grotesque."

Then there were peals of riotous laughter, ill-bred as only that of men and women whom etiquette habitually controls; the revolt of a long thraldom, the protest of fashion against rule. The ultra-civilized must have his holiday when the pristine animal wakes up, to howl and grin, uncaged and free.

Fainter and fainter grew their voices, more and more distant the reverberations of their derision. But they had been careless. Peering through the creepers, her hands upon her temples, a million scorpion tongues let loose to lash her ears! What! they all! Pitted against one! Powerful, self-possessed, cynical! And but the one at bay! fettered, insignificant, "grotesque"—she—*she*—had said it! In that quick birth of time before the mirthful echo of their laughter died on her ears, before she dragged herself into the house, Beth had traversed the narrow verge which separates hatred from crime.

CHAPTER XVIII

They strolled across the gardens, heedless, merry. They settled on the terrace. From Mrs. Bush's false ambitions which found expression in monkey tricks of futile imitation, they fell to discussing the various elements which compose the elective association called society.

"I like my own dear, dull, insipid set the best," Arden was saying, decapitating poppyheads as she talked, with probing parasol. "We know each other's grip masonic, we understand each other. I can chaff my intimates, rebuke and snub them. They return the compliment in kind, and generously. No evil is intended, no offense taken. We abuse each other roundly, then kiss and come to tea. All is clear. I have had my vision of Bohemia, and have taken a flyer now and again into that realm, and oh! how gladly have I crept back to our Philistine ranks, all torn up, bitten, and ashamed! When I walk and am tired, I don't care to rest on a wasp's nest. Of the inhabitants of Bohemia, only the real ones are interesting. Most of them are half-and-halfs, and these are intolerable. A *manqué* man or woman of the world is deplorable, but a *manqué* Bohemian is far worse. He lacks sincerity. Oh, I've had the craze for sad-eyed female poets and for geniuses of the tattered coat. We have all been there. It's picturesque. But the fact is they're just like ourselves, without our amiability and with a million times more conceit. And one never can say the right word to their self-worship; they are never satisfied. The nicer we are to them the more they blackguard us. They are always 'disappointed' in our entertainments, surprised to find our gowns unbecoming, our houses stuffy, our manners abominable. They sigh. They had looked for better things. The sad-eyed poet is touchy. She asks if our women friends intended to slight her, our men to be over-familiar. Every topic bristles with dangers, every word must be weighed. *A la fin* such commerce is . . . irksome."

"The people who provide the music for others to dance by are always blackguarded," said Mr. Isham. "Their energy is considered frivolous. Even Horace has his little fling at the entertainers. They amuse

Mæcenas too splendidly, he thinks. To me they seem unselfish."

"I never tried any other set but our own," said a young married lady who had driven some miles for a call, "because it would bore my husband." She began to give her opinions of life in general and of husbands in particular. Her own hated serious people only liked sporting men and larky women. So she humored him. She never denied him anything . . . anything within reason, and the society which pleased him. That was the only way to keep a man.

"I think the only way to keep a man quiet," she was saying, "is never to deny him any physical pleasure."

"Eh? What?" said Mr. Isham, staring, with his hand at his ear.

"I put down my opera box and footman last winter—such hard times, you know—that Blunt might have his hunters. He must have his exercise. Men must be exercised and amused or they get drinking and frolicking."

There was something impersonal and extremely naïve in these revelations of conjugal theory. Impersonal and absolutely devoid of vanity. One felt, she thought she or another could do it as well; conduct an orderly household, give good dinners, see that the husband got his gallop.

She was tall, with the figure and unconscious movements of a handsome boy. Her smile was full of childish explanations. She had pretty blown brown hair, and large round eyes, iridescent like soap bubbles seen in candlelight. If these eyes were not charged with mystery or danger they were at least honest. She impressed one with her honesty. She informed the company that she read all the books that were worth reading as quickly as they could be printed, but that she never spoke of their contents to her husband lest he should be fatigued. Men could not be expected to take an interest in women's pursuits. Mrs. Blunt had an answer ready for every timeworn riddle, but how to keep a husband was, she thought the most important one. While she elaborated her resources in this direction—which were doubtless ample and fruitful—Arden Ayrault yawned at stated intervals with unblushing openness. She had not kept her husband. If report spoke truly, somebody's else wife was keeping him, and Arden thought it just as well. She had separated from him some years before. The mere remembrance of the man wearied her. All those things which had torn her life had happened so long ago that they brought mental lassitude. Light discourse could never reach or touch them any more. She had a sense of unreality as to her past.

"Dear me," said she, "and how long *can* a man be kept constant on this régime? One craves instruction."

"I should say that one might keep a man with these methods until he was seventy," said Mrs. Blunt, with conviction.

"But women grow old and ugly," ventured Lola.

"My dear, don't get so easily discouraged," said Arden, mischievously. "Diane de Poitiers allured three generations, and Helen of Troy was forty-six when she set towns on fire."

"Fancy!" said Lola.

"In these days of Babcock extinguishers the fire would be put out before it ever went to history, and the poor Helens get no credit."

"I read in Ninon de l'Enclos's Memoirs that she had a lover of eighty-four," said Mrs. Blunt.

"I think it was horrid of her then," said Lola. "Forty breaks most women's hearts. I should think by eight-four that organ would be pretty well battered."

"Well, I'm seventy," said Mr. Isham,

"and mine is not completely damaged yet."

"How can the heart be kept young?" sighed Arden.

"Don't over-eat, don't be envious, and never backbite," said the artist.

"Genius has no age," said Lola to him, "but when I am old, who have no talents, only affections, I want an old dead heart. It would be so dreadful to love without requital."

"By the way, is May Plunkett going to marry that Western Colonel?" asked the practical Mrs. Blunt.

"I should think he was much too old for her," said Lola.

"Tut, tut," said Mr. Isham. "If she is what I take her for, Miss Plunkett likes her own way. Let her take her lover of fifty then. There's nothing so mulish as a boy. Men of fifty have occasionally blundered, are conscious of some failures, but the young fellows have no such handicaps. Why at twenty I was as obstinate as a pig. Odious. Well, now I'm seventy"—he rose and drew up to the wood fire, turning his back to the flame, and warming his hands under his coat-tails—"I look upon quinquagenarians as mere lads. Ha! ha! So it goes! So it goes!" And he laughed, and wheezed, in genial contentment.

"What the ladies like is ardor," said the Count. "Women like men who take them seriously."

"Is that the reason they coddle Asch?" said Mr. Marston, maliciously. "Hang it, if I've ever been able to account for what women did like or dislike."

"Ah, a man is more than a god or less than a man with the ladies," said Mr. Isham, "according to their sweet caprice."

"One cannot say," said the Count, reflectively, "that *l'ami* Asch is *entreprenant.*"

To the Frenchman full of enthusiasm and of blood, a temperament which no mood of gayety, no game of personal interest, no titillation of vanity, no gust of passion ever seemed to sway or to excite was an enigma profoundly repulsive, yet withal interesting. He had watched Fenno Asch as the Latins watch, with keen critical acumen whetted by distrust. His distrust he found groundless. Asch's habitual and general incivility turned out to spring from no enmity, but from the impassive indifference which ground ambassadors in the same mortar as ordinary people, but which otherwise did not interfere with them. The young man's absence of all reverence disarmed de Beaumont's suspicion that he intended to be impolite, pushed by that twinge of jealousy, envy, or manly rivalry so common among his own people. de Beaumont had studied him carefully. He knew that to Fenno Asch the trump of an archangel would have seemed no more than the blast of a penny whistle, the rush of his mighty wing no greater than the flutter of barnyard feathers. Before the loveliness of the loveliest woman he knew the young man could remain without dream as without desire, while the favors of an empress would have left his heart cold and his head clear. The Frenchman was torn, in his contemplation of this peculiar temperament which belittles all things, between hot scorn and genuine admiration.

"I should kill myself if the man I loved wearied of me," Lola was saying to Arden, who followed Mr. Isham's lead and enlarged on the fickleness of immature affections.

"O, my dear, I daresay," she replied, with the mellow laugh which often belied her words and puzzled the dull-witted. "You are capable of just such silliness. What's the use, will you tell me, of letting him survive to have a nice time? *Du reste*, my love, a man who had once tasted of your sweetness and who could get tired of it would not be fit to live an hour. His career had better be closed at once. He would be a dog." She spoke jestingly, but with spirit and meaning. Lola blushed furiously, she knew not why. Marston nodded at his wife, smiling. He seemed to say to her:

"I'm all right. I'm a faithful husband. Don't worry. I'm faithful."

"Bless me if he is n't reassuring her," thought Mr. Isham, and chuckled to himself. His host's fatuity always diverted him. It is to be surmised Mrs. Marston was grateful. There are moods, however, when women need less to be assured about the sentiments they inspire than about those which they experience. When they throw out tentacula in that direction it is unfortunate that man's obtuseness rarely offers them the needed aliment. The artist had sometimes seen a wistful look in Lola's eyes which had gone through his tough heart.

"Why does n't he fall at her feet?" he would ask himself with the ingenuousness of the man who is n't married.

Archie ran in just then with his inseparable friends and followers, the mastiffs and the collie. He sat upon a stool, at his mamma's bidding, and drank a cup of milk, and nibbled a piece of cake with aristocratic daintiness, and his father, when he looked at him, trembled with joy and pride, the joy and pride of his own prowess. His love for his little boy was very real. He called him to his side, and pulled his curls, and poked him in the ribs, and played with him as perhaps the butcher may have played with his own offspring. Archie laughed and screamed with delight, and spilled his milk and was not scolded for it.

By-and-by they scattered to rest or read in their own apartments, and later to array themselves for the cheerful feasting and music of the evening hour.

When Lola bade her husband good-night, she said to him:

"People seem to enjoy themselves here, dearest. They like our home as much as we do. I am sure I hope they are comfortable. Kiss me."

Then quiet fell on the silent terraces, a brooding stillness on the stately villa. Everything slept. Not a sound swept the night under its heaven of stars; but about two o'clock a change crept over the weather. Gusts of wind seemed suddenly let loose, to beat and scream, and whirl about the eaves.

Pierre Rose sat up and listened. Sat up in his bed away in the servant's wing. He awoke from a dream of love. His lips had been glued to a pair of lips the wish for whose possession had lately haunted him.

Pierre was a man of the world and something of a cynic, but his dreams were far less cool than his tenets. He awoke to find the ivy which grew close to his window sweeping long beckoning fingers across its pane, from which a recreant shutter had blown back upon the gale. He awoke to find outside a wind-swept darkness, and within a sense of cold, of desolateness, and —what was still more terrible—a toothache. To awake from a warm kiss to a toothache!

"What have I done?" thought Pierre, groaning and tossing on his bed, "that the Lord should so *s'acharner à moi?*"

Pierre was a serious person, and in his way a believer. He was not much of a dreamer when once well awake. Earth was earth to him, as it is to most philosophic Frenchmen; neither heaven or hell; a good enough place if one could only keep one's heart and one's self free from too many complications, earn one's bread, pay one's debts, and lay up something for old age.

Now he loved, and his love was decidedly a complicated one. He was not at all sure that he would suit the young lady, and he was perfectly certain that she did not suit him. Her name was Floribel Pullen. On that very afternoon he had met her in the woods, and had presented her with a locket which had belonged to his mother. This lady had been given to lockets. She had been a celebrity of the concert cafés, and had danced and sung to the Parisian public for many years. She had as much jewelry as she had lovers, and such of her trinkets as had not been sold to defray the expense of masses for her repose of soul were still owned by her son. For this son she was ambitious. She intended him for the priesthood. Was this a lurking expiatory aspiration which the lad might thus vicariously fulfill? Should he rebel, she at least hoped to make of him a doctor. Once, however, in a sharp moment of poverty, when she had sulked herself out of engagements, and out of lovers, she apprenticed him as a mirmiton to an Italian restaurant. This sealed his fate. He developed a culinary genius so remarkable that it settled his destiny. He was one of those lucky individuals whose talent orders fate.

Now his income was larger than that of the average country clergyman or lawyer. He was happy in his work, grateful to his mamma for having allowed him to follow his own bent. He managed to enshrine the poor woman's memory in an aureole of filial reverence that her ill-concealed secrets, which had poisoned his youth, could not dispel. Floribel Pullen had admired the dangling gem upon his watch-chain, and Rose had promptly severed it with his pocket-knife and laid it at Circe's feet. Floribel accepted the gift, offered half in jest. She was one of those women who accept . . . everything; but with such affable acknowledgment that a man must feel himself the debtor still.

He doubted if he would suit her, because he knew that the word "servant" meant in Paradise a brand of immeasurable opprobrium. He had not forgotten his reception at Mrs. Bush's. Miss Pullen would certainly not accord favors to a cook whom it was probable she would decline to marry.

Rose for years had caressed the hope of himself opening a restaurant which should rival the great ones of Paris and of New York. Like all wise Frenchmen, thrifty in his expenses, he had laid up money. The hope was fast ripening into a decision. Towering above this refectory planed an image of serene womanhood. He would take a wife the day he opened its doors. But one element was eliminated from his purposes. The disturbing mischief-making God of Love, that imp of mischiefs and misdemeanors, was to be exorcised. If Anteros was not to be of the banquet, even Eros was superfluous. He knew himself capable of respect and tenderness toward a wife.

These he thought would suffice. From a stronger sentiment he shrank in fear. Now, tossed on his pillow by the sting of physical suffering, he felt himself penetrated by that other anguish at once so sweet and so ensnaring. Floribel! She, whom he had heard called light a hundred times! She, whom he barely respected, and loved only with that fierce desire of the senses which he felt should be eliminated from prudent marriages. Floribel Pullen! What a helpmeet! Frivolous Floribel! vain Floribel! whom he adored just because she was so frivolous and so vain. He groaned and turned upon his bed, a toy to that masterpassion in which all resolve, like all sagacity, crumbles and lies crushed.

Pierre was a quiet, sensible, decent fellow, but Floribel Pullen had laughed into his eyes on the day of Mr. Marston's speech, and since that hour he had known no peace. Now, all unnerved, he got up to fasten the flapping shutter, whose rasping rattle yet more excited his overwrought fancy. He raised the window and looked out. The night, in spite of the windstorm, was white and clear. Upon the horizon were those strange rays of yellow light of which one asks if they are a memory of the sun-setting or a herald of the dawn. The senescent moon had vanished. Her waning trailed a gleam, illuminating the heavens.

Lolling for a moment at the casement, Rose became aware of a furtive flutter beneath him, of a step upon the gravel, a breath, a sign of human nearness. Over the country, save for the fitful wind, deep silence reigned. With the strained eye and ear which darkness lends to us, he rather guessed than saw and heard a presence. Yes—here—there—no doubt any more—he caught distinctly the waving of a garment, a long, light cloak flung out for a moment against the gale. The first impression of his excited brain was that Floribel had come to him . . . at last, that in a moment he would be beside her, that he would bear her in his arms to shelter, and that there she would shyly, yet willingly, nestle upon his breast. Extremely intelligent, of a nature more wary than impulsive, the flood of rapture that the hope brought him, the thirst for her presence which it awakened, warned the young man decisively of where he stood. At the same moment a painful twinge from his aching tooth sent the tears into his black eyes—

"*Sacré bleu! Sacré tonnerre!*" he exclaimed angrily, carrying his hand to his cheek with the plaint of self-pity. The flitting female figure had vanished; not, however, before he perceived it was not Floribel's. Whose then? The height, the walk, the movement of the head had shown—Beth Bush. But where one has not seen the features, who can be certain? There are things we know of which nevertheless we fain would be made sure. If it indeed were she, what did she here—alone? on this cold night? In her arms it had seemed to him she bore some bundle. What? Something intangible, feathery, weightless; it had half flown from her and there against a tree was lingering, entwining, beating about the trunk. What was it?

"*Sacré tonnerre!*"

He shoved down his window and went to a small chest, from which he extracted a vial of laudanum. From this he soon dropped upon cotton, torn from his leathern jewel-box, a few red drops and placed them in his mouth. Beth or another, he did not care. Curious he was, no doubt, but not to the extent which pushes investigation. He was suffering too much. Perhaps it was one of the maids after all, belated in the village, letting herself in through some carelessly latched aperture. Yet it had seemed to him the farmer's wife. It did not occur to him to imagine in her nocturnal errand evil intent, and certainly not one of amorous intrigue. He laughed at the mere thought. Whatever she might be, her thin-lipped virtue, the man felt, was secure. Rose was a passable judge of character. He rarely made mistakes. Who could tell? Perhaps she had heard the distant bleat of a lambkin forgotten by the shepherd in the meadow, and had come out to bring it to the fold.

The fumes of the drug when once again he sought his couch, dulled alike wonderment and pain. He sank into heavy sleep. From this, two hours later, he was suddenly startled. His arm was almost roughly shaken, two wild, frightened eyes looked into his, while slender nails pierced the flesh above the elbow. They were those of his mistress.

"Pierre—Pierre!" she was saying, hurriedly. "Quick, quick, my good Pierre, awake, awake! Fire! fire!"

Already, as he sat up, staring, he heard her light step through the hall from sill to sill, and her voice calling:

"Augustine—Mary-Ann—Jane—François—fire! fire! fire! Marie—Philip—fire!"

And through the corridors the words were taken up with cries of terror and dismay. Some had locked doors; others, like Pierre, left theirs ajar; some slept hard—it took longer to rouse them—but on and on she sped, a winged Rhamnusia awaking the slothful from their besotted slumbers, swift-footed, ghostlike—

"Awake, awake, be vigilant! Fire! fire! fire! danger is nigh!"

CHAPTER XIX

Very early Lola, who slept lightly, had been awakened by a curious sound. It reverberated in her half-wakened mind with a throb of fear. She listened, startled. Some one was in her room! She sprang from her bed, fumbled for a match, struck it. It flared, illuminating the vast apartment from carpet to ceiling. Its spark snapped, and went out between her trembling fingers. Nothing! Yet stealthily creeping, creeping, like a skulking creature crawling along the floor, yes, more and more distinctly, now at hand, almost under her feet, this strange movement, this unearthly warning. What was it?

"Jock — Rip — Victor," she whispered, coaxingly, thinking perhaps a miscreant mastiff was ramping, ambushed, behind some convenient screen, and shrank from banishment. But to her call came no response. And now as she stood there, paralyzed, motionless, another of her senses started to consciousness. She drew quick little breaths into her quivering nostrils, and with it an odor tingling, peppery, as of something charred and singed. Hastily enveloping herself in her dressing-gown, with lighted candle now, she hurried across the parquet. What was that? lazily curling up close to her desk? Twisting its serpent way between her and the struggling dawn, indolent, impalpable, a thin white vapor rose and coiled, and louder, louder, louder, the creeping grew, shivered, moaned like the plaint of some imprisoned being panting for freedom. As she paused an instant with distended pupil, the vapor widened, darkened, then flamed with a sudden reddish hue. To her frightened fancy it seemed to assume demoniac shapes, hostile and maleficent.

She knew then that her room was on fire. Her first impulse was toward her husband, her second to her child. Which—which? She craved the care of the one, the other was so helpless! Was it selfishness which took her first to Mr. Marston, or was it self-reproach that for an instant she had wavered? Ah! she still loved him best, she told herself, as she laid her hand upon his arm.

Shaken from one of those deep slumbers which drug the energies and will, she found it hard to stir him, to make him understand.

"What? What?"

The others were more quickly roused.

Fenno Asch, easily wakened, was the last to appear. He sent for his valet, ordered all of his belongings carefully rescued and packed, made a comfortable toilet—there is a tradition that he shaved—after which he lit a cigarette, and leisurely joined de Beaumont on the lawn. The latter was arrayed in a pink silk bed-quilt, and was holding helplessly in his arms a bust of that motherly person who is called the Venus de Milo. He had swung the goddess from her pedestal as he ran from his apartment, already filled with smoke and rocked by falling timbers.

Mrs. Ayrault and some of the servants had formed a fire brigade outside with Mr. Marston, who, in pajamas, a top hat, and one slipper, was handling a hose with praiseworthy persistence. His figure loomed against the flames which issued from the ballroom.

The French maid, Augustine, away in the further wing where no danger for at least an hour could reach her, pushed by the force of a dramatic nature, was hurling her garments out of the window. Gowns, hats, ribbon, petticoats, fluttered eastward, lodged in trees and adorned neighboring bushes, while she herself wildly gesticulated, weeping loudly.

An Irish laundress was praying in the kitchen, crossing herself in invocation to all the saints and to the Blessed Virgin Mother, while her young assistant was pulling at her gown, hysterically imploring her to flee from impending destruction.

Pierre Rose, after organizing a company of the fast-arriving villagers, bidding them do all they could to save from the lower floors their valuable contents—the upper rooms were already impassable—vanished.

Bush, early on the premises, worked valiantly with Ackerman and the farmhands. They had been warned by the alarm bell. François, the maître d'hôtel, robed in a flowing nightshirt, was dragging pictures, silver, books, and porcelains, helter-skelter through the open windows.

"Rose, Rose," he called, missing the young Frenchman's energetic helpfulness. "Where can he have gone?"

Leaping over obstacles, gasping, breathless, Pierre was running toward the cottage where once before he had been so unwelcome a visitor. Its door was half ajar, and now it did not close upon him, but gave way to his nervous hand. In the narrow passage, unwashed, uncombed, disconsolate, loudly sobbing, stood . . . Dottie.

"What is the matter, little one?" said

Pierre, taking hold of the child's ear, and looking about him furtively while he drew her against his knees. Dottie, in spite of her mother's protests, entertained a secret admiration for Rose, and his confectionery. She now explained to him with loud weeping how everybody had gone to the fire—her mother, and even the perfidious Jane—but that she, under some frightful threat of punishment, had been forbidden to move, and all this frantic fun going on and she left out!

"Oh! oh! oh!" she shrieked, at the mere thought of her wrongs. "The house will be all burned up, and I'll never—oh, Mr. Pierre, I'll never see even the pretty big light. I can't! Ma said I was n't to stand out on the porch even, and—oh! oh! oh!

Rose mastered his temptation to shake her, and hearkened for a moment to her ramblings.

"Look here, petite," he said to her, "where is your mother?"

Dottie assured him that she did not know.

"Is she over at the big house?"

She had gone out, and that was all her daughter could communicate.

"Now, chérie," said Rose, quickly, "where is your mother's room?"

The child puzzled, but somewhat pacified

by Rose's exciting presence, pointed up the narrow stairs.

"Petite," said the chef in a low voice, "will you go upstairs and get me a pair of your mother's boots?"

"Did ma send for them?" asked Dottie, eying him suspiciously.

"Bless me, yes," said Pierre. "She's got her feet wet with the pumps."

"You said you had n't seen my ma," said Dottie with astuteness.

"Blank the little Yankee," thought Pierre. "She might be a *Juge d'instruction*."

"You misunderstood me, little dear." He smiled, while inwardly consigning Dottie and her family to ten thousand devils to destroy. "Your mother sent me for her boots. I was only joking."

"If I get the boots will you ask her if I can come out and see the fire?" said the commercial Dottie.

"Why of course I will. I will come back in a few moments with her permission to bring you."

"Hang it, if I don't throw the little baggage in and broil her," thought the Frenchman, at the end of his indulgence.

Slowly, and looking backward at him, as if to make sure the contract was not a cheat and lie, Dottie brought him a pair of her mother's boots, still dusty with sand, and delivered them to him from her little brown hands. Pierre took and eyed them with a peculiar gleam in his black eyes. He concealed one of them under his coat as he walked away, tossing the other from him over the hedge.

"One is enough," he said audibly.

A little later he could be seen kneeling upon the gravel which stretched under his windows, first here, then there. Ah! here, wound about a tree-trunk, in the wind something yellow tossed and flapped. Rose gave vent to a cry of triumph when he had pulled a handful of straw from about a gnarled root. Yes, again he knelt, and by-and-by uttered another stifled exclamation. He had found what he sought! Quickly Beth's boot sprang from its hiding-place; it fitted, heel and toe, width and length, into a footprint which, with several others of like size and shape, was plainly marked on the soft soil. Pierre Rose looked grave when he arose from his recumbent attitude.

Fenno Asch, faultlessly dressed, meandered up to Lola, where she stood with Archie and his nurses, below the terraces, watching the burning of her home. She met him with the chill and cutting light of a pale glance from under haughty eyelids.

With murmured words she could not catch, he turned on his heel and left her abruptly.

Mr. Isham had performed prodigies in saving articles of value. The Count, while less efficient, and impeded by his bed-quilt, had fought the fire-god with equal bravery. Asch alone saved . . . himself and his effects. Lola, revolted, inwardly vowed he had slept his last sleep under a roof of hers.

The flames, shooting forth in ever-increasing volume from the consuming pile, now reached the portico. Their red tongues played about an ornament, a bit of sculptured carving above the columns. Hit by a piece of loosened masonry, its graceful efflorescence wavered a moment, then fell with a crash, its hot débris scattering their ruins upon the path. A curious recklessness seemed suddenly to inundate Mrs. Marston's mind, almost a sense of pleasure.

"See, Archie, see," she said to her son; "now the columns will give way. Ah! there is mamma's room.all fallen in. See, Archie, see! And my piano, that must be gone. Ah, Augustine! Where are my jewels? In their case? My pearls and opal coronet? And my coats—the sable one—that too? Did it hang in the vestibule? And my poor little bird? Is that dead? Did they save that, do you think?

She ran hither and thither, fascinated. The sparks fell on her hair. She wished that she had more to burn, more to throw upon the general pyre, that she might bring to this great conflagration all her possessions. She tore a scarf from off her neck, and cast it on the wind, and watched it toss against the crumbling walls and feebly scorch itself to dust. Her spirit felt detached from all material things. The intoxication of their destruction was in her veins.

The villagers had grown a trifle weary; they were piling the saved things into farm-wagons and driving them across the lawn to the "Colony." The wine cellar had been sacked. Some of the men waxed hilarious, Two were quite drunk, quarrelsome, noisy. Others exchanged witticisms as they passed each other with their self-imposed freight. They forced themselves to gravity only when they met the master, or cried "hist" when they fancied one of "the family" remarked their cheerfulness. Sympathy is fatiguing. Consternation gave place to indifference. There was almost a note as of orgy in the air, and all the while the great and splendid flame swept across the desolate country, bearing down everything in its track.

It was just then that "Crazy Jim" came down upon the scene.

What village, or what county, but has its "Crazy Jim?" He sought shelter and a meal now and then in the poorhouse, but most of his days and nights were spent upon the roads, singing or cursing, as the mood of his whisky was mild or virulent. To-day he was in glee. His peaked hat all awry, his face aglow. How did he get into the house? How scale the stairs? No one could tell. They saw at the window his furfuraceous visage lighted up with exultation, his drooling mouth distended by wild laughter. He began to throw things down, mattresses, pillows, tables, chairs.

"Ha! ha! ha!"

Here was a costly china vase. He cast it on the sward. It struck and broke. He clapped his hands in rapture.

"Ha! ha! ha!"

The emancipation of his cowed nature whipped his blood to frenzy! He would have liked to bray and brag of his importance and his services. Mrs. Marston had been kind to him. He was glad he had arrived in time. But soon they who were watching saw there was no retreat for Jim. Behind him swelled the dense, black pall, before him—death. Well, well, why not? What was his life worth? His mean and cowardly and driveling life?

"My God! my God!" cried Lola. "He is doomed! He is lost! O, God, have mercy on his soul! Poor Jim! Poor Jim!"

The women who surrounded her, Mrs. Fesser, Mrs. Opdyke, Mrs. Bryan, Mrs. Pullen, joined in lament and outcry.

Pierre Rose heard. In a moment he placed the saving ladder. Like a cat, he sprang from rung to rung, seized the madman by the beard, stunned his struggles with a blow, and on his shoulders bore him down to safety.

It was just then that Floribel, fresh from her morning bath, in her best hat and Sunday jacket, with sorrowing eyes and sweet condolence, joined Mrs. Marston's group. Rose, surrounded by the lauding women, was blowing on his blackened hands. Their eyes met.

CHAPTER XX

Piled up with wreckage, the "Colony" presented, some hours later, an odd appearance. In its tiny sitting-room Lola was resting, sipping some tea with little Archie and Mrs. Ayrault. The other guests had all departed in various trains, and thus relieved her of their presence. She and Arden were discussing the fire, but with a certain languor, as a thing long ended, already relegated to the past.

In an office across the hall three men were closeted. They were Pierre Rose, Mr. Marston, and the sheriff. Pierre's hands were bandaged. Mr. Marston was flushed at the cheek-bones, and appeared agitated. The sheriff was sucking a pipe, and now and then shooting a stream of brown liquid from between his teeth. Sometimes this struck the hearth at which it was aimed, and sometimes it did not.

"I guess," he was saying, "the testimony is fairly conclusive if Mr. Rose is willing to take his oath."

"What period of time," asked Mr. Marston, "is included in the night season?"

"Well, I guess between the sun-setting and the sun-rising," said the sheriff, scratching his head.

"It was two o'clock. I had a toothache. I got up. I looked at my watch," said Pierre.

"If you can prove a motive . . ."

"It seems difficult," said Mr. Marston.

"In the day time, second degree. First degree is imprisonment for term not less than fifteen years; second, not more than ten; third degree, seven years. Just had a case up on Mount Ararat, third degree. Man put up for seven years, if I remember."

"As I understand, it is the malicious destruction of any building, house, or other institution capable of affording shelter to human beings."

"Ex-actly," said the sheriff, dividing his assent by a hyphen of ejected saliva.

"The boot fitted into the footprint. I saw the straw in her arms—later around on Madame's side, I found some more of it, which the wind had carried to the terrace. She set it under the wooden rail. The tempest it was high," said Pierre.

"Did not arson bear the death penalty formerly?" said Mr. Marston, with blood in his eye.

"Now I can't say but it did—sometime back," said the sheriff. "It's a common-law felony, that's a fact, but nowadays it's dealt with more mildly."

"Hanging is too good for such creatures," said Mr. Marston. "They ought to be . . ."

"If she can't prove an alibi, and you prosecute, I guess it'll go hard with her."

"What looks to me decisive is her disappearance—this trumped-up summons to Pontifex, their old home, just at the hour of the fire, and her departure while it was in progress, professedly to her aunt's sick-bed; her forsaking Mrs. Marston and her duties at such a sad moment. I have an assurance from the telegraph operator that no telegram was received."

"I guess she warn't very smart," said the sheriff. "Do you suspect anybody on the premises of complicity? Husband? Eh? They ain't ever smart at their first offense; get flustered. What beats me is what they had to gain . . . hem . . . hem."

"*Non, Monsieur, non, non,*" said Rose, with fervor. "*Monsieur Bush est un honnête homme.*"

"What does he say? Eh? My French is getting rusty," chuckled the sheriff. "I never was much on foreign tongues."

"He believes in Bush's honesty, integrity, and I must say," said Mr. Marston, "I do myself. Mrs. Marston thinks highly of him."

"Been informed?"

"Not yet, poor wretch," said Mr. Marston, uneasily. "Not yet. We must prepare our case."

"Guess you'd better trot him around here," said the sheriff.

"Will you break it to him?"

"I shan't beat around the bush, if that's what you mean. I guess he's got to hear the truth, and the sooner it's out the better for all parties concerned."

"There's no hurry."

"Well now, I guess there is," said the sheriff. "We don't want no grass growin' under our feet. If we can catch him in his talk it may make things lively. Jog 'em up a little. This ain't the first little operation of the kind I've performed this year. I guess I can stand it if he can." And the sheriff chuckled again.

It was then that Mr. Marston went and called his wife, and that she was initiated into the pregnant secrets of the conclave.

Unknowing of the storms which had ravaged Elizabeth's heart and brain, the whole thing was to her incredible. There are characters which must be studied in entirety to be understood. Fragmentary knowledge of them is insufficient. The little comprehension she had gained of Mrs. Bush's nature hardly accounted for the transformation of a fretful scold into a mentally disturbed and desperate pyromaniac. The abrupt cataclysm which could hurl Beth to such depths of infamy appeared apocryphal, a fairy tale. The thought of Joseph filled her with apprehension and distress, and it was tearfully she begged her husband to temper, as far as in him lay, to the man's simple, loyal soul, the horrid blow that must be dealt to him.

Joe was washing his hands and face, and preparing to rest from his labors when he received a summons about nine o'clock that his presence was desired at the Colony. He had worked very hard all of the day with the determination to help his employers to the uttermost. He had himself put Dottie to bed, and was preparing to seek his own lonely couch. His wife's sudden incomprehensible départure filled him with surprise and with consternation, and if no glimmer of the truth dawned upon his mind it was restless and disquieted enough to be prepared for shock.

Waking in the night he had missed her from his side. He had dozed, and when she returned she complained of indisposition, of sleeplessness, and had told him that she had been resting in the spare room. As to the occurrences of the morning, Jane's and Dottie's accounts did not seem to agree. Soon after he reached the scene of calamity the former had brought him a verbal message from his wife to the effect that she had but five minutes wherein to reach the stage from Paradise to the railway station, that she has received a call to her aunt's at Pontifex where illness made her presence imperative, that she must catch the first train cityward, and feared delay should she go to say good-bye to him in person. Mrs. Bush had further given Jane directions as to the men's supper and as to keys. When questioned as to how and when the Pontifex summons had arrived, Jane became flurried, but she was positive that Mrs. Bush had worn her traveling dress, had taken a small handbag and some money, and had walked away toward the stage stables. These minor details had escaped the eye of the only daughter of the house of Bush. To her nothing had been confided. She was told to be a good girl and stop in the house, and she supposed her mamma was going over to the big house to see it burn. Filled with the woe of her own disappointment, Dottie had seen no handbag, no money, and even her mother's costume left but a dim impression. Yet she thought she wore her dark dress. Later, Dickson, the stage driver, who lounged over to hear the news, admitted having conveyed Mrs. Bush to the station, and having seen her board the early train. With his tongue in his cheek, Joseph laboriously penned a postal to his wife—he feared telegrams as sure portents of death—and sent it to the afternoon mail by the shepherd lad. Queries as to the particulars of her strange flight, as to her aunt's condition, and accounts of the fire were compressed into the limited space in disconnected phrases. To doubt her truth never crossed his brain, but he felt that her methods had been unusual and upsetting. His heart, however, was so full of sympathy for Mr. and Mrs. Marston, the sight of the smoking ruins of their home so pained him that he was fain in their misfortune to forget his own annoyance. He thought Elizabeth should not have left in such a crisis, and certainly not without a word with her husband, but he told himself in a future hour all would be explained. Her aunt had been a mother to her; she owed her duty.

At Mr. Marston's summons he now hastily wiped his hands, and, instead of his bed, sought the Colony. The sheriff, absent for several hours, had now returned by appointment. He was already in Mr. Marston's office. It took a long while to make the unfortunate man understand his position, and the rôle his wife was supposed to have played. Perhaps Mr. Marston would have been more than human had not the words felony, fifteen years of prison, death penalty, rolled over his tongue with a certain unction, but it took time before Joe comprehended that his wife was accused of arson, and he was expected to tell what he knew. When he fully realized that he must defend her, and perhaps himself, from so heinous and terrible a charge, the expression of his face became so pitiable that Pierre Rose instantly repented of his part in the affair, that Mr. Marston grew fidgety, and even the sheriff looked uncomfortable. He was asked pointblank if Mrs. Bush had gone out in the night, and he said "yes," and then contradicted himself and said "no," and finally took refuge in silence. Then he asked, looking about helplessly, that a lawyer might be sent for, for him to consult with.

"You can have all the lawyers you want, Mr. Bush, when your case comes up," said the sheriff, kindly. "This is only a preliminary unofficial kind of a chat among friends, and they ain't going to take any undue advantage of you."

"You don't expect a man to testify against his wife, and the mother of his little one?" asked Joe, huskily. "Mebbe there's them as thinks they has cause to hate her, as bears a grudge, 'll do it quick enough."

Pierre winced.

"Justice will be done," said Mr. Marston, severely.

"And I think," went on Joe, looking at Pierre, "that them as tries to hurt an innocent woman and a little child ain't much of men either—not according to my lights. But Satan knows his children," he added, under his breath, "and 'll claim 'em all in his own good time."

"Of course, Mr. Bush, you are perfectly confident of Mrs. Bush's innocence," said the sheriff, blandly. "You understand, we ain't pressing you to change your opinion, which may be well founded. We have got two witnesses and the evidence of the footprints. One of the farm hands saw Mrs. Bush out on the path between the dwelling-house and cottage at about three A. M. His name is Thomas Shannon. He sleeps over the barn, I'm told. He rose to shut his window from the storm."

The three men put their heads together

and whispered. Like a creature at bay Joe looked from one to the other of his persecutors, for such they seemed to his distorted fancy. Their net was drawing round him. Unflinching as he was in rectitude, he had always been slow to believe evil of others, but now the mists began to scatter. Percival Oakes, Elizabeth, their strange talks, her disaffections, her suppressed angers, her almost morbid self-control—were these the early signs of madness? The madness that had killed her father? His head fell forward on his breast, and he remained plunged in profound reflection. By-and-by, when the three had done their talk, as if some sudden resolve possessed him, he arose and stood before them, pointing upward with one hand as if to command attention.

"I have to ask of these present," he said, solemnly, " a favor. I have a confession to make, but I will make it to Miss Marston, and I ask to see her alone."

Mr. Marston thought Mrs. Marston had gone to her much-needed rest, and could not be disturbed at present.

"I can wait till morning," said Joe, "but if it were so as she ain't retired I'd like a word with Miss Marston to-night."

Lola expressed herself willing to receive him upstairs, in the room where she was lying on a lounge while the maids prepared a bed for her. She motioned to them to leave her and Bush alone when he had stumbled up the stairs. She tried to speak cheerfully to him, but the words died on her lips when a lamp had been found and she saw the man's face. It was livid. His eyes' habitual melancholy had deepened into anguish.

"My poor Joseph," she murmured, half inaudible.

He came up to where she lay, still holding his battered straw hat between his fingers, and he, too, tried to speak, but could not. She was shaken by the pathos of his lonely figure.

"My poor Bush," she repeated. "This is indeed terrible, but remember we exonerate you entirely."

"I guess when ye know the truth it ain't me as ye'll exon'rate." He repeated her word. "Can I speak with ye for a moment?" As she looked up astonished: "I had n't never been with such folks as you was, Miss Marston, and I wan't used to their ways. In Pontifex we was all alike, and there warn't no lookin' up or down, but all of us equal and like one big family. Here it was different. Mr. Marston, he found great fault with me, and I got riled. He accused me and my folks of things we never thought was wrong, and what with one thing or another the devil got into my soul. P'raps I got covetous. I was angered and sore, and, Miss Marston, I—'t wan't my Elizabeth that plotted the destruction of your beautiful home. She thought too much of ye. She never was tired of talking of ye before ever she set eyes on ye. Why, she was that set on coming to live in this place I had to give in for peace's sake. I say"—he again raised his arm above his head impressively—"she's innocent. I come to confess my guilt. I done it! I done it! I done it! As God hears me, Miss Marston, and you hope for His forgiveness in the world we're all going to, my Elizabeth's innocent. I done it!"

The last word rang out wildly through the silent room. Lola had listened earnestly to these incoherent utterances, to this resolve to suffer vicariously for her for whom it now was plain the man would willingly give his life. Yet those truth-loving lips were as if shriveled with the lie they told. They had grown pale and harsh, and his tongue was parched and dry in the ecstasy of his excitement.

"Why do you tell me this?" said Lola, almost sternly.

"The first time ever I seen ye, Miss Marston, when my wife asked me if you was a reg'lar beauty, I told her there was handsomer women, p'raps, but yours was the sweetest face ever I looked on. So, somehow, to-night, in my misery, I thought maybe it would be easy to . . . to . . . tell it all . . . ask ye . . ." He broke down then and fell into a chair, sobbing, beating the air impotently with outstretched hands.

In a moment they were imprisoned fast in Lola's slender ones, their rough palms pressed in passionate pity upon her breast. As she held them close, and bent over them, all the nobility of his ignorant hope, of his futile desire to shield the wretched woman who was to-day, not only the mother of his child, but a great criminal, swept her soul, and as upon the perfumed sweetness of her white bosom his head rested, for a moment, all its weight of weariness and sorrow, Lola cried out to him, throwing one arm across his shuddering shoulders, cried out across the waste of life—" Oh, my brother! "

Outside the night crept on apace. It enveloped alike the toad which burrows earthward, the bat which swirls and swoops in the dark, the owl which hoots in the tree, and the bird which sings to the stars. It fell over the land, and inclosed it tenderly; ardent, sombre, full of dreams.

CHAPTER XXI

Mr. Isham stood at his easel. He was finishing May Plunkett's portrait. He was dissatisfied. The hour of travail with the artist is his hour of joy. His delivery that of discouragement. The true artist is an exile. He sighs for something lost, or left behind, promised but never reached, toward which he wanders with bleeding feet; and sometimes he would fain lie down in the desert, curse God and die.

A knock at his door roused him from unpleasant contemplation. Usually impatient of interruption, he hailed this morning anything which would distract him from his present mood.

"I am getting old," he said to himself. "My day is over." And a pang unknown before to his philosophy left its sting in his heart. And this day, which was over, had it really ever dawned? Perhaps not. He was inclined to think he had never amounted to much. He would have done better to have been a banker's clerk as his father had wished, or an engineer. He might by this time have become one of those men who in England are Prime Ministers, and in the United States bank presidents or railroad "magnates."

"I should at least have had some money," he grumbled, but his grumbling to-day had in it a note of suffering. "No, probably I should not. I'm incidental. At best a respectable mediocrity. I should have remained a clerk on two thousand a year. To dirty canvas was my only alternative, but even that was not a vocation. Lemuel Isham, make no mistakes."

"Come in."

The door swung open. A young man entered. There was a certain assurance in his manner. If this young man had a vocation, one felt sure he would recognize it. Possibly might mistake instincts for inspirations, tendencies for talents, tastes for commands direct from heaven.

"Where have I seen this gentlemanly, shabby, clever-looking chap before?" thought Mr. Isham, puckering his eyebrows, and glaring at the intruder with a snort, over his spectacles.

"Your face is familiar," he said. "Where have I seen you before? I've got a poor memory for names."

"My name is Oakes."

"Eh? Eh? Oakes, did you say?"

"I doubt, sir, if you ever saw me before in your life, but I've seen you a great many times."

"Well, Mr. Oakes, I'm glad to meet you. How can I serve you? Sit down, sit down."

"I've seen you many times, and what's more I know your works. As I can respect talent when I find it, you will pardon me for telling you that of the crowd who visited Marston Terrace you always seemed to me the only person of the whole gang worth looking at twice."

"Humph!" said Mr. Isham.

The slightly patronizing tone of his unknown visitor, with the conceit which deems its opinion of value, struck the old gentleman as distinctly diverting.

"You probably never saw or heard of me, although I stood sometimes in the mud when you splashed by with Marston and his friends."

"Indeed! Well, I do n't know about splashing you. I always remark the side of the street we are not on looks the cleanest, but when we have crossed over it's all about the same. But I have seen your face, and now I remember your name. Were not you the schoolmaster in Paradise?"

"I was."

"I have heard of you, and I can tell you exactly now what I heard."

Mr. Oakes laughed a trifle unpleasantly. "That I was a revolutionist, who frightened all the old women?"

"Not at all! That you were a fool."

"You're frank, at least."

"Thanks. I can lie as well as anybody when it's necessary, but it is a bad habit and softens the brain."

"And I guess yours isn't soft yet."

"My brain isn't worth discussing, particularly in the morning when, as you see, I'm busy. Did you ever pass this young lady, eh? Did she ever splash you in the ... er ... gang? Step up here, Mr. Oakes, and tell me what's the matter with her, eh?" He put his hand upon Oakes's arm and twisted him to a stand before the easel whereon Miss Plunkett faintly smiled. Oakes's gray eyes dwelt intently on the picture.

"It's the form and features of a girl I've often seen, but you have given her, Mr. Isham, the soul of another woman."

"Eh? Eh? What did you say? What did you say? Speak louder. I'm a little deaf," said Mr. Isham, gruffly.

"I think you heard me," said Oakes.

"Perhaps the other lady occupied your mind. The form, the features, the high coloring are the girl's—I don't know her name—the eyes are Mrs. Marston's."

"Damn it!" muttered Mr. Isham. "But I believe the fellow's right. The fair Lola had got hold of me and bedeviled me with her sweet witcheries."

"Do you know Mrs. Marston?" he asked, abruptly. There was a moment's silence.

"No," said Oakes. "I do not know her." He could not have explained the impulse, born no doubt of some refined ancestry, which made him disclaim acquaintance with the mistress of Marston Terrace. The fine soul of the old artist perhaps dimly understood his delicacy. He had heard of Oakes, and now recalled that Mrs. Marston had spoken of him kindly, and had even told him some story of an encounter with the young man in a wood on a night of storm.

"How can I serve you?" he now repeated more courteously. "Pray sit down, sit down," and blowing his nose, and wheezing, he pushed a stool fussily forward, and seated himself upon another. Lounging was not a rule of his atelier.

"Plague on my bronchitis!" he said under his breath.

Oakes had a roll of papers under his arm, and produced them.

"I called upon you this morning, Mr. Isham, for two reasons. The first was to ask you some particulars of the Marstons' fire. The second, to speak about a personal matter. First, then, will you tell me—I can gather nothing from the newspapers—if Mrs. Marston and her little boy escaped quite unhurt from the flames, quite?" He leaned forward, eagerly, clasping his hands just below two rusty but well-brushed creases at the knees of his trousers.

"I was down there when the calamity occurred. I saw everybody safely out: Mr. and Mrs. Marston, and the boy. Nobody was injured. Yes—I make a mistake—the cook, Rose, burned his hand, I believe, while rescuing a crazy tramp, who somehow got upstairs."

"And she—Mrs. Marston—is well? you are sure? I . . . was sorry for *her*—"

Something in the young man's voice, a vibration, a tremor, caused Mr. Isham to scan him narrowly.

"It was hard lines. Yes, they were very comfortable. Mrs. Marston caught a cold, so she tells me, has coughed ever since. I have a letter I got this morning. The ladies stood out too long in the wet grass. They were half clad."

"And Mrs. Marston looks to be delicate. She could ill bear such exposure. The shock alone was terrible for one like her. I wished I might have been there . . . to . . . to . . ."

Again Mr. Isham looked hard at the speaker.

"Mrs. Marston was very well taken care of," he said, a little dryly, "of course."

There was a pause.

"What was the origin of the fire?"

"There are various theories," said Mr. Isham, vaguely, as if he knew far more than he was willing to communicate. "I am not at liberty to speak."

"Why, what *can* you mean?" The intensity of Oakes's manner seemed over-accentuated for the natural query.

"Perhaps," said Mr. Isham, with meaning, "the Marstons had enemies."

"Why, why, Mr. Isham, is there a supposition that there was incendiarism?"

"And sometimes our enemies are they of our own household."

Oakes paled. A sudden, strange surmise had crossed his mind.

"It could only be a deed of madness."

"Possibly; but I will ask you to let even the little I have dropped go no further. The family have decided not to prosecute. I mean—I mean, not to investigate."

"Ah!"

"Mrs. Marston is a generous woman."

"I believe you." Again the young man's manner betokened some inward tumult.

Mr. Isham turned the subject. "And now what are these papers?"

"These papers, sir, are some essays I have written."

"Indeed!" Mr. Isham smiled grimly.

"They dwell on and describe the lives and the homes of the wretched, of the oppressed. I have also taken up the cause of woman," and as Mr. Isham threw up a deprecating arm: "I know the ladies you frequent, sir, decry female agitators. Do they appreciate that all their present ease is the result of the effort of this much vilified sisterhood? It was not the satisfied and lazy ones who wrung reform from man's unwilling brutishness. They now enjoy what the others have died for, and in their pampered folly insist it is enough. But the mills of the gods go on. I thought I would ask you to look over these essays, hoping you might consent to illustrate them with your pencil. Am I very bold?"

"Well, yes, rather. I don't do that sort of thing."

"I once saw some sketches of yours, done when you were young, in a collection, in an exhibition . . ."

Mr. Isham leaned back in his seat and gave way to one of his lusty roars.

"Some ass kept those, did he? Well, I was n't much of a success at first. Munson the great man then, told me I'd better give up, that I never should draw. My father, I remember, blessed him. But I was pig-headed. How the bookmakers do detest the race-horse to be sure who bolts every course as a two-year-old, and manages to win in his fifth year. People never forgive us whose predictions of failure we nullify. Ha! Ha! Ha!"

He seemed to have left behind his phase of despondency, and to have, through some reminiscence, been roused to high good-humor. Pessimism is character, not philosophy or belief. Mr. Isham was not a pessimist.

"The obstacles, the want of support from friends, from family, then, did not cripple you?" asked Oakes, with earnestness. "You think there is hope for the lonely souls?"

"The nightingale only chirps when he is

with his mate. It is when he is away from her that he sings," said the old man, a little sadly.

That ephemeral beauty which Mrs. Marston had remarked in him suddenly transfigurged the schoolmaster's pale face, and gave it radiance. It did not escape the eye of the painter.

"I could take your hand for that, Mr. Isham!" he exclaimed.

"And so you wish me to look over these?" The old man turned over the leaves of the manuscript, not unkindly.

"If you will. You understand a few sketches of yours would be to me of immeasurable value, but I don't ask favors. It's not a habit of mine. If the work is not worth your trouble—"

"Tut! tut! Young man, you go too fast. What I can't understand is why you came to me at all."

This indeed was a mystery which Oakes himself had barely solved. Might it be the eternal answer, that Mr. Isham was not the rose, but had lived near her?

"Well, I will look over these, and see you another day." And as Oakes parted from his papers somewhat gingerly and anxiously: "I'll not lose them. Do not be afraid," he said, smiling.

"This work is my ewe lamb," said Oakes. "I hope it may make me famous. I have only the one copy from my notes."

"So you want and hope for fame?"

Something in Percival Oakes, which had for a moment touched Lola's imagination in the wood-cabin, something of nobility and of exaltation, piercing his moroseness, his discontent, and his conceit, awakened Mr. Isham's interest.

"Yes," said Oakes.

"And you expect it?"

"They told you I was a fool, but it's not true. I'm no fool, and I'll prove it to them."

"Who do you mean by they?"

"The people who crush us."

"Whew!"

"I had to express myself or die."

"That is right. It is better to express one's self than to die. It is always better to speak out. Better to quarrel than to murder." It was Oakes's turn to laugh.

"Sometimes the two are synonyms."

"Not always. It is repression that makes the criminals."

"Mr. Isham," said Oakes, "if there were more men of your wit the world would be a better place."

"I don't know about that. I've been

outwitted very often. The world's good enough. Oh, I know there are rich and there are poor, children die, friends grow cold, lovers betray, envy pursues success, malice and treachery are rife, and all the rest of it. Very bad, very bad, of course. But since struggle seems to be the law of life, let us meet it like heroes, and not like knaves or cowards. Those antique fellows fought destiny, the romantics were after their tyrants; we moderns fight passions and morals, and our hearts and brains are the seat of battle. Now you, I daresay, have a grievance, and you have aired it in your book. If it is clever it will bring you a lot of fun, and if it is not, it has at least given you some pleasant hours and a healthful occupation. All this you will say is a selfish view, for I infer you desire to help humanity. It seems to me I have heard as much. Well, I hope you may. It's a difficult job, but not impossible. You certainly will do so by cultivating cheerfulness in yourself. Then if your book is a success, you will assist the publisher. Mrs. Publisher will get some new bonnets, and the five little Publishers new velocipedes. I wish you luck. You won't put much money in our own pocket, but you will be benefiting your neighbor. Good-day, good-day, Mr. Oakes; come again, come again. I will be glad to see you." And the old man, with his good-natured satire, conducted the young man to his door.

. . . . .

This was Lola's letter:

. . . " Archibald and the sheriff and Rose think there was a good case, but I could not stand the husband's humiliation. I just could not. He took it all on himself. He was so noble. I will tell you about it some day. It seems there are angels left in the world. Rose says it was all envy, that she went almost crazy because she was not something else—like Arden, perhaps. Arden always turns everybody's head. But how extraordinary! We laughed at her the last time we went up to the cottage the day before the fire. It was horrid of us, but even if she heard, how could such a trifle turn her brain? Still I blame myself. I might have been kinder, but she was so absurd. Archibald says I am a goose, and that she ought to be hanged. Bush and the child have left, and I hear they found her near Pontifex, somewhere at an inn. What a meeting! But that man is godlike! I wonder if she confessed to him. But of course her disappearance was confession. Was it remorse, or fear? It was not at all clever, at any rate, was it? She must be just a little mad. I hear they are going to the West. Poor creatures! I can't help pitying her. She seemed such a proud woman. Here it is hushed up. No one knows, and no one shall. I simply dragged myself around on my knees to Archibald until he promised not to do anything. Perhaps it wasn't a very strong case for us after all.

"Apropos, of Rose—who insists she did it—he is going to leave us. You won't get any more of his delicious *bouillabaise*. He is going to be married, and to whom do you think? But you won't remember her. She sat next to us at that terrible political thing when poor Archibald—but, after all, I believe you were not there, thank God! Her name is Floribel Pullen. The neighbors say she has been wicked, that she is very sly, and over-fond of the gentlemen! I can't believe it. She is candor itself, and most attractive. It seems it's a great passion, and so no more fish soup for us. I hope he will be happy. He was a good fellow. She was fascinated by his heroism about Jim. The question is, does he deserve happiness for saving Jim's life? Jim *is* such a nuisance! Archibald thinks he might better have burned up.

"I got a chill that morning and am

poorly. I cough all the time. I look quite pulled and hollow-eyed. The doctors say my left lung is a wee bit weak. We sail next week on the 'Moravia.' We shall be gone a year or more. I feel depressed. I think I must be ill. I shall seek the sun. Come and see us off."

THE END.

PRINTED AT THE LAKESIDE PRESS
FOR HERBERT S. STONE & CO.
PUBLISHERS, CHICAGO

THE PUBLICATIONS OF HERBERT S. STONE & CO. THE CHAP-BOOK The HOUSE BEAUTIFUL

CAXTON BUILDING, CHICAGO
111 FIFTH AVENUE, NEW YORK
1897

CAXTON BUILDING, CHICAGO
111 FIFTH AVE., NEW YORK

THE PUBLICATIONS OF HERBERT S. STONE & CO. THE CHAP-BOOK The HOUSE BEAUTIFUL

Ade, George.

ARTIE: *A Story of the Streets and of the Town. With many pictures by* JOHN T. MCCUTCHEON. *16mo.* $1.25.
Ninth thousand.

"Mr. Ade shows all the qualities of a successful novelist."—*Chicago Tribune.*

"Artie is a character, and George Ade has limned him deftly as well as amusingly. Under his rollicking abandon and recklessness we are made to feel the real sense and sensitiveness, and the worldly wisdom of a youth whose only language is that of a street-gamin. As a study of the peculiar type chosen, it is both typical and inimitable."—*Detroit Free Press.*

"It is brim full of fun and picturesque slang. Nobody will be any the worse for reading about Artie, if he does talk slang. He's a good fellow at heart, and Mamie Carroll is the 'making of him.' He talks good sense and good morality, and these things have n't yet gone out of style, even in Chicago."—*New York Recorder.*

"Well-meaning admirers have compared Artie to Chimmie Fadden, but Mr. Townsend's creation, excellent as it is, cannot be said to be entirely free from exaggeration. The hand of Chimmie Fadden's maker is to be discerned at times. And just here Artie is particularly strong—he is always Artie, and Mr. Ade is always concealed, and never obtrudes his personality."—*Chicago Post.*

"George Ade is a writer, the direct antithesis of Stephen Crane. In 'Artie' he has given the world a story of the streets at once wholesome, free, and stimulating. The world is filled with people like 'Artie' Blanchard and his 'girl,' 'Mamie' Carroll, and the story of their lives, their hopes, and dreams, and loves, is immeasurably more wholesome than all the stories like 'George's Mother' that could be written by an army of the writers who call themselves realists."—Editorial, *Albany Evening Journal.*

Ade, George.

PINK MARSH: *A Story of the Streets and of the Town. With forty full-page pictures by* JOHN T. MCCUTCHEON. *16mo. Uniform with Artie.* $1.25.

Fourth thousand.

"There is, underlying these character sketches, a refinement of feeling that wins and retains one's admiration."—*St. Louis Globe-Democrat.*

"Here is a perfect triumph of characterization. * * * Pink must become a household word."—*Kansas City Star.*

"These sprightly sketches do for the Northern town negro what Mr. Joel Chandler Harris's

'Uncle Remus Papers' have done for the Southern old plantation slave."—*The Independent.*

"It is some time since we have met with a more amusing character than is 'Pink Marsh,' or to give him his full title, William Pinckney Marsh of Chicago. * * * 'Pink' is not the conventional 'coon' of the comic paper and the variety hall, but a genuine flesh and blood type, presented with a good deal of literary and artistic skill."— *New York Sun.*

"The man who can bring a new type into the literature of the day is very near a genius, if he does nothing else. For that reason Mr. George Ade, the chronicler of 'Artie,' the street boy of Chicago, did a rather remarkable thing when he put that young man into a book. Now Mr. Ade has given us a new character, and to me a much more interesting one, because I do not remember having met him face to face in literature before.—*Cincinnati Commercial Tribune.*

Benham, Charles.
The Fourth Napoleon: *A Romance.* *12mo. $1.50.*

An accurate account of the history of the Fourth Napoleon, the *coup d'état* which places him on the throne of France, the war with Germany, and his love intrigues as emperor. A vivid picture of contemporary politics in Paris.

Bickford, L. H.
(and Richard Stillman Powell.)
Phyllis in Bohemia. *With pictures and decorations by* Orson Lowell, *and*

a cover designed by FRANK HAZENPLUG. *16mo. $1.25.*

Sentimental comedy of the lightest kind. It is the story of Phyllis leaving Arcadia to find Bohemia, and of her adventures there. Gentle satire of the modern literary and artistic youth and a charming love story running through all.

Blossom, Henry M., Jr.

CHECKERS: *A Hard-Luck Story. By the author of "The Documents in Evidence." 16mo. $1.25. Tenth thousand.*

"Abounds in the most racy and picturesque slang."—*New York Recorder.*

"'Checkers' is an interesting and entertaining chap, a distinct type, with a separate tongue and a way of saying things that is oddly humorous."—*Chicago Record.*

"If I had to ride from New York to Chicago on a slow train, I should like a half dozen books as gladsome as 'Checkers,' and I could laugh at the trip."—*New York Commercial Advertiser.*

"'Checkers' himself is as distinct a creation as Chimmie Fadden, and his racy slang expresses a livelier wit. The racing part is clever reporting, and as horsey and 'up to date' as any one could ask. The slang of the racecourse is caught with skill and is vivid and picturesque, and students of the byways of language may find some new gems of colloquial speech to add to their lexicons."—*Springfield Republican.*

Bloundelle-Burton, John.

ACROSS THE SALT SEAS: *A Romance of the War of Succession.* By the author of "*In the Day of Adversity,*" "*The Hispaniola Plate,*" "*A Gentleman Adventurer,*" etc. *12mo.* $1.50.

In "The Hispaniola Plate" Mr. Burton showed his familiarity with the stories of the buccaneers of the Spanish Main. In this new story there is still this picturesque element, although the scene is the battle of Vigo and the looting of the Spanish galleons. The hero escapes through Spain in an attempt to reach Marlborough in Flanders, and has many exciting though not improbable adventures. Any one who cares for good fighting, and in whose ears the "sack of Maracaibo" and the "fall of Panama" have an alluring sound, will like the book. There is also an attractive love story in a rather unusual form.

Chap-Book Essays.

A VOLUME OF REPRINTS FROM THE CHAP-BOOK. *Contributions by* T. W. HIGGINSON, H. W. MABIE, LOUISE CHANDLER MOULTON, H. H. BOYESEN, EDMUND GOSSE, JOHN BURROUGHS, NORMAN HAPGOOD, MRS. REGINALD DE KOVEN, LOUISE IMOGEN GUINEY, LEWIS E. GATES, ALICE MORSE EARLE, LAURENCE JERROLD, RICHARD HENRY STODDARD, EVE BLANTYRE SIMPSON, and MAURICE THOMPSON, *with a cover designed by* A. E. BORIE. *16mo.* $1.25.

Chap-Book Stories.
A VOLUME OF REPRINTS FROM THE CHAP-BOOK. *Contributions by* OCTAVE THANET, GRACE ELLERY CHANNING, MARIA LOUISE POOL, *and Others. 16mo.* $1.25. *Second edition.*

The authors of this volume are all American. Besides the well-known names, there are some which were seen in the *Chap-Book* for the first time. The volume is bound in an entirely new and startling fashion.

Chatfield-Taylor, H. C.
THE LAND OF THE CASTANET: *Spanish Sketches, with twenty-five full-page illustrations. 12mo.* $1.25.

"Gives the reader an insight into the life of Spain at the present time which he cannot get elsewhere."—*Cincinnati Commercial Tribune.*

"Mr. Chatfield-Taylor's word-painting of special events—the bull-fight for instance—is vivid and well colored. He gets at the national character very well indeed, and we feel that we know our Spain better by reason of his handsome little book."—*Boston Traveler.*

"He writes pleasantly and impartially, and very fairly sums up the Spanish character. * * * Mr. Taylor's book is well illustrated, and is more readable than the reminiscences of the average globe-trotter."—*New York Sun.*

Chatfield-Taylor, H. C.

>THE VICE OF FOOLS: *A Novel of Society Life in Washington. By the author of "The Land of the Castanet," "Two Women and a Fool," "An American Peeress," etc. With ten full page pictures by Raymond M. Crosby. 16mo. $1.50.*

The great success of Mr. Chatfield-Taylor's society novels gives assurance of a large sale to this new story. It can hardly be denied that few persons in this country are better qualified to treat the "smart set" in various American cities, and the life in diplomatic circles offers an unusually picturesque opportunity.

D'Annunzio, Gabriele.

>EPISCOPO AND COMPANY. *Translated by Myrta Leonora Jones. 16mo. $1.25. Third edition.*

Gabriele d'Annunzio is the best known and most gifted of modern Italian novelists. His work is making a great sensation at present in all literary circles. The translation now offered gave the first opportunity English-speaking readers had to know him in their own language.

De Fontenoy, The Marquise.

>EVE'S GLOSSARY. *By the author of "Queer Sprigs of Gentility," with decorations in two colors by* FRANK HAZENPLUG. *4to. $3.50.*

An amusing volume of gossip and advice for gentlewomen. It treats of health, costume, and entertainments; exemplifies by reference to noted beauties of England and the Continent; and is embellished with decorative borders of great charm.

Earle, Alice Morse.

CURIOUS PUNISHMENTS OF BYGONE DAYS, *with twelve quaint pictures and a cover design by* FRANK HAZENPLUG. *12mo.* $1.50.

"In this dainty little volume Alice Morse Earle has done a real service, not only to present readers, but to future students of bygone customs. To come upon all the information that is here put into readable shape, one would be obliged to search through many ancient and cumbrous records."—*Boston Transcript.*

"Mrs. Alice Morse Earle has made a diverting and edifying book in her 'Curious Punishments of Bygone Days,' which is published in a style of quaintness befitting the theme."—*New York Tribune.*

"This light and entertaining volume is the most recent of Mrs. Earle's popular antiquarian sketches, and will not fail to amuse and mildly instruct readers who love to recall the grim furnishings and habits of previous centuries, without too much serious consideration of the root from which they sprang, the circumstances in which they flourished, or the uses they served."—*The Independent.*

Embree, Charles Fleming.
> For the Love of Tonita, and Other Tales of the Mesas. *With a cover designed by* Fernand Lungren. *16mo.* $1.25.

Characteristic and breezy stories of the Southwest, by a new author. Full of romantic interest and with an unusually humorous turn. The book coming from a new writer, is likely to be a real surprise. The cover is an entirely new experiment in bookbinding.

Fletcher, Horace.
> Happiness as found in Forethought minus Fearthought, and other Suggestions in Menticulture. *12mo.* $1.00.

The enormous popularity of Mr. Fletcher's simple philosophy, as shown in the sale of his first volume, "Menticulture" is a sufficient evidence of the prospects of the new book. In it he develops further the ideas of menticulture and urges with energy and directness his plea for the avoidance of worry.

Fletcher, Horace.
> Menticulture: *or the A-B-C of True Living. 12mo.* $1.00.
> *Nineteenth thousand.*

Transferred by the author to the present publishers.

Gordon, Julien.
> EAT NOT THY HEART: *A Novel. By the author of " A Diplomat's Diary," etc. 16mo, $1.25.*

Life on Long Island at a luxurious country place, is the setting for this story, and Mrs. Cruger's dialogue is as crisp, as witty, as satirical of the foibles of fashionable life as ever. She has tried a new experiment, however, in making a study of a humbler type, the farmer's wife, and her ineffectual jealousy of the rich city people.

Hapgood, Norman.
> LITERARY STATESMEN AND OTHERS. *A book of essays on men seen from a distance. 12mo. $1.50.*

Essays from one of our younger writers, who is already well known as a man of promise, and who has been given the unusual distinction of starting his career by unqualified acceptance from the English reviews. Scholarly, incisive, and thoughtful essays which will be a valuable contribution to contemporary criticism.

Hichens, Robert.
> FLAMES: *A Novel. By the author of " A Green Carnation," " An Imaginative Man," " The Folly of Eustace," etc., with a cover design by* F. R. KIMBROUGH. *12mo. $1.50. Second edition.*

"The book is sure to be widely read."—*Buffalo Commercial*.

"It carries on the attention of the reader from the first chapter to the last. Full of exciting incidents, very modern, excessively up to date."—*London Daily Telegraph*.

"In his last book Mr. Hichens has entirely proved himself. His talent does not so much lie in the conventional novel, but more in his strange and fantastic medium. 'Flames' suits him, has him at his best."—*Pall Mall Gazette*.

"'Flames,'" says the *London Chronicle*, in a long editorial on the story, "is a cunning blend of the romantic and the real, the work of a man who can observe, who can think, who can imagine, and who can write."

"'Flames' is a powerful story, not only for the novelty of its plot, but for the skill with which it is worked out, the brilliancy of its descriptions of the London streets, of the seamy side of the city's life which night turns to the beholder; but the descriptions are neither erotic nor morbid. * * * We may repudiate the central idea of soul-transference, but the theory is made the vehicle of this striking tale in a manner that is entirely sane and wholesome. It leaves no bad taste in the mouth. * * * 'Flames'—it is the author's fancy that the soul is like a little flame, and hence the title—must be read with care. There is much brilliant epigrammatic writing in it that will delight the literary palate. It is far and away ahead of anything that Mr. Hichens has ever written before."—*Brooklyn Eagle*.

James, Henry.

WHAT MAISIE KNEW: *A novel. 12mo.* $1.50.

The publication of a new novel—one quite unlike his previous work—by Mr. Henry James, cannot fail to be an event of considerable literary importance. During its appearance in the *Chap-Book*, the story has been a delight to many readers. As the first study of child-life which Mr. James has ever attempted, it is worth the attention of all persons interested in English and American letters.

Kinross, Albert.

THE FEARSOME ISLAND; *Being a modern rendering of the narrative of one Silas Fordred, Master Mariner of Hythe, whose shipwreck and subsequent adventures are herein set forth. Also an appendix, accounting, in a rational manner, for the seeming marvels that Silas Fordred encountered during his sojourn on the fearsome island of Don Diego Rodriguez. With a cover designed by* FRANK HAZENPLUG. *16mo. $1.25.*

Le Gallienne, Richard.

PROSE FANCIES: *Second series. By the author of "The Book-Bills of Narcissus," "The Quest of the Golden Girl," etc. With a cover designed by* FRANK HAZENPLUG. *16mo. $1.25. Second edition.*

"In these days of Beardsley pictures and decadent novels, it is good to find a book as sweet, as pure, as delicate as Mr. Le Gallienne's."—*New Orleans Picayune.*

"'Prose Fancies' ought to be in every one's summer library, for it is just the kind of a book one loves to take to some secluded spot to read and dream over."—*Kansas City Times.*

"There are witty bits of sayings by the score, and sometimes whole paragraphs of nothing but wit. Somewhere there is a little skit about 'Scotland, the country that takes its name from the whisky made there'; and the transposed proverbs, like 'It is an ill wind for the shorn lamb,' and 'Many rise on the stepping-stones of their dead relations,' are brilliant. 'Most of us would never be heard of were it not for our enemies,' is a capital epigram."—*Chicago Times-Herald.*

"Mr. Le Gallienne is first of all a poet, and these little essays, which savor somewhat of Lamb, of Montaigne, of Lang, and of Birrell, are larded with verse of exquisite grace. He rarely ventures into the grotesque, but his fancy follows fair paths; a certain quaintness of expression and the idyllic atmosphere of the book charm one at the beginning and carry one through the nineteen 'fancies' that comprise the volume."—*Chicago Record.*

Magruder, Julia.

MISS AYR OF VIRGINIA, AND OTHER STORIES. *By the author of "The Princess Sonia," "The Violet," etc. With a cover-design by* F. R. KIMBROUGH. *16mo.* $1.25.

"By means of original incident and keen portraiture, 'Miss Ayr of Virginia, and Other Stories,' is made a decidedly readable collection. In the initial tale the character of the young Southern girl is especially well drawn; Miss Magruder's most artistic work, however, is found at the end of the volume, under the title 'Once More.'"—*The Outlook.*

"The contents of 'Miss Ayr of Virginia' are not less fascinating than the cover. * * * These tales * * * are a delightful diversion for a spare hour. They are dreamy without being candidly realistic, and are absolutely refreshing in the simplicity of the author's style."—*Boston Herald.*

"Julia Magruder's stories are so good that one feels like reading passages here and there again and again. In the collection, 'Miss Ayr of Virginia, and other stories,' she is at her best, and 'Miss Ayr of Virginia,' has all the daintiness, the point and pith and charm which the author so well commands. The portraiture of a sweet, unsophisticated, pretty, smart Southern girl is bewitching."—*Minneapolis Times.*

Malet, Lucas.

THE CARISSIMA: *A modern grotesque. By the author of " The Wages of Sin," etc. 12mo. $1.50. Second edition.*

*⁎*This is the first novel which Lucas Malet has written since "The Wages of Sin."

"The strongest piece of fiction written during the year, barring only the masters, Meredith and Thomas Hardy."—*Kansas City Star.*

"There are no dull pages in 'The Carissima,' no perfunctory people. Every character that goes in and out on the mimic stage is fully rounded, and the central one provokes curiosity, like those of that Sphinx among novelists, Mr. Henry James. Lucas Malet has caught the very trick of James's manner, and the likeness presses more than once."—*Milwaukee Sentinel.*

"The interest throughout the story is intense and perfectly sustained. The character-drawing is as good as it can be. The Carissima, her father, and a journalistic admirer are, in particular, absolute triumphs. The book is wonderfully witty, and has touches of genuine pathos, more than two and more than three. It is much better than anything else we have seen from the same hand."—*Pall Mall Gazette.*

"Lucas Malet has insight, strength, the gift of satire, and a captivating brilliance of touch; in short, a literary equipment such as not too many present-day novelists are possessed of."—*London Daily Mail.*

"We cannot think of readers as skipping a line or failing to admire the workmanship, or to be deeply interested, both in the characters and the plot. 'Carissima' is likely to add to the reputation of the author of 'The Wages of Sin.'"—*Glasgow Herald.*

Merrick, Leonard.

One Man's View. *By the author of "A Daughter of the Philistines," etc. 16mo. $1.00.*

The story of an ambitious American girl and her attempts to get on the English stage, her marriage and subsequent troubles, and the final happiness of every one. The author's point of view and the story itself are unusual and interesting.

"Very well told."—*The Outlook.*

"Clever and original."—*Charleston News and Courier.*

"Eminently readable."—*New Orleans Times-Democrat.*

"A highly emotional, sensational story of much literary merit."—*Chicago Inter Ocean.*

"A novel over which we could fancy ourselves sitting up till the small hours." — *London Daily Chronicle.*

"A really remarkable piece of fiction * * * a saving defense against dullness that may come in vacation times."—*Kansas City Star.*

Moore, F. Frankfort.
The Impudent Comedian and Others. *Illustrated. 12mo. $1.50.*

"Several of the stories have appeared in the *Chap-Book*; others are now published for the first time. They all relate to seventeenth and eighteenth century characters — Nell Gwynn, Kitty Clive, Oliver Goldsmith, Dr. Johnson, and David Garrick. They are bright, witty, and dramatic.

"Capital short stories."—*Brooklyn Eagle.*

"A thing of joy."—*Buffalo Express.*

"The person who has a proper eye to the artistic in fiction will possess them ere another day shall dawn."—*Scranton Tribune.*

"Full of the mannerisms of the stage and thoroughly Bohemian in atmosphere."—*Boston Herald.*

"The celebrated actresses whom he takes for his heroines sparkle with feminine liveliness of mind."—*New York Tribune.*

"A collection of short stories which has a flash of the picturesqueness, the repartee, the dazzle of the age of Garrick and Goldsmith, of Peg Woffington and Kitty Clive."—*Hartford Courant.*

"The stories are well conceived and amusing, bearing upon every page the impress of an intimate study of the fascinating period wherein they are laid."—*The Dial.*

"Mr. 'F. Frankfort Moore had a capital idea when he undertook to throw into story form some of the traditional incidents of the history of the stage in its earlier English days. Nell Gwynn, Kitty Clive, Mrs. Siddons, Mrs. Abington, and others are cleverly depicted, with much of the swagger and flavor of their times."—*The Outlook.*

Moore, F. Frankfort.
THE JESSAMY BRIDE: *A Novel. By the author of " The Impudent Comedian."* 12mo. $1.50.

A novel of great interest, introducing as its chief characters Goldsmith, Johnson, Garrick, Sir Joshua Reynolds, and others. It is really a companion volume to "The Impudent Comedian." The first large English edition of "The Jessamy Bride" was exhausted before publication. The great popularity of his other books is sufficient guaranty of the entertaining qualities of this latest volume.

"Admirably done."—*Detroit Free Press.*

"It is doubtful if anything he has written will be as well and as widely appreciated as 'The Jessamy Bride.'"—*Kansas City Times.*

"This story seems to me the strongest and sincerest bit of fiction I have read since "Quo Vadis."—George Merriam Hyde in *The Book Buyer.*

"A novel in praise of the most lovable of men of letters, not even excepting Charles Lamb, must be welcome, though in it the romance of Goldsmith's life may be made a little too much of for strict truth * * * Mr. Moore has the history of the time and of the special circle at his fingerends. He has lived in its atmosphere, and his transcripts are full of vivacity. * * * 'The Jessamy Bride' is a very good story, and Mr. Moore has never written anything else so chivalrous to man or woman."—*The Bookman.*

Morrison, Arthur.

A CHILD OF THE JAGO. *By the author of "Tales of Mean Streets." 12mo.* $1.50. *Second edition.*

"The book is a masterpiece."—*Pall Mall Gazette.*

"The unerring touch of a great artist."—*London Daily Graphic.*

"Told with great vigour and powerful simplicity."—*Athenæum.*

"Remarkable power, and even more remarkable restraint."—*London Daily Mail.*

"A novel that will rank alone as a picture of low-class London life."—*New Saturday.*

"The power and art of the book are beyond question."—*Hartford Courant.*

"It is one of the most notable books of the year."—*Chicago Daily News.*

"'A Child of the Jago' will prove one of the immediate and great successes of the season."—*Boston Times.*

"The description of the great fight between Josh Perrott and Billy Leary is a masterpiece."—*Punch.*

"Never, certainly, a book with such a scene on which so much artistic care has been lavished. * * The reader has no choice but to be convinced."—*Review of Reviews.*

"Mr. Arthur Morrison has already distinguished himself (in his *Tales of Mean Streets*) as a delineator of the lives of the East-end poor, but his present book takes a deeper hold on us."—*London Times.*

"Is indeed indisputably one of the most interesting novels this year has produced. * * One of those rare and satisfactory novels in which almost every sentence has its share in the entire design."—*Saturday Review.*

"Since Daniel Defoe, no such consummate master of realistic fiction has arisen among us as Mr. Arthur Morrison. Hardly any praise could be too much for the imaginative power and artistic perfection and beauty of this picture of the depraved and loathsome phases of human life. There is all of Defoe's fidelity of realistic detail, suffused with the light and warmth of a genius higher and purer than Defoe's."—*Scotsman.*

"It more than fulfills the promise of 'Tales of Mean Streets'—it makes you confident that Mr. Morrison has yet better work to do. The power displayed is magnificent, and the episode of the murder of Weech, 'fence' and 'nark,' and of the capture and trial of his murderer, is one that stamps itself upon the memory as a thing done once and for all. Perrott in the dock, or as he awaits the executioner, is a fit companion of Fagin condemned. The book cannot but confirm the admirers of Mr. Morrison's remarkable talent in the opinions they formed on reading 'Tales of Mean Streets.'"—*Black and White.*

Powell, Richard Stillman.
(See Bickford, L. H.)

Pritchard, Martin J.
WITHOUT SIN: *A novel.* *12mo.* $1.50.
Third edition.

*⁎*The New York *Journal* gave a half-page review of the book and proclaimed it "the most startling novel yet."

"Abounds in situations of thrilling interest. A unique and daring book."—*Review of Reviews* (London).

"One is hardly likely to go far wrong in predicting that 'Without Sin' will attract abundant notice. Too much can scarcely be said in praise of Mr. Pritchard's treatment of his subject."—*Academy.*

"The very ingenious way in which improbable incidents are made to appear natural, the ingenious manner in which the story is sustained to the end, the undoubted fascination of the writing and the convincing charm of the principal characters, are just what make this novel so deeply dangerous while so intensely interesting." — *The World* (London).

Pool, Maria Louise.
IN BUNCOMBE COUNTY. *16mo.* $1.25.
Second edition.

"'In Buncombe County' is bubbling over with merriment—one could not be blue with such a companion for an hour."—*Boston Times.*

"Maria Louise Pool is a joy forever, principally because she so nobly disproves the lurking theory that women are born destitute of humor. Hers is not acquired; it is the real thing. 'In Buncombe County' is perfect with its quiet appreciation of the humorous side of the everyday affairs of life."
—*Chicago Daily News.*

"It is brimming over with humor, and the reader who can follow the fortunes of the redbird alone, who flutters through the first few chapters, and not be moved to long laughter, must be sadly insensitive. But laugh as he may, he will always revert to the graver vein which unobtrusively runs from the first to the last page in the book. He will lay down the narrative of almost grotesque adventure with a keen remembrance of its tenderness and pathos."—*New York Tribune.*

Raimond, C. E.

THE FATAL GIFT OF BEAUTY, AND OTHER STORIES. *By the Author of "George Mandeville's Husband," etc. 16mo. $1.25.*

A book of stories which will not quickly be surpassed for real humor, skillful characterization and splendid entertainment. "The Confessions of a Cruel Mistress" is a masterpiece, and the "Portman Memoirs" exceptionally clever.

Rossetti, Christina.

MAUDE: *Prose and Verse. With a preface by William Michael Rossetti. 16mo. $1.00.*

THE CHAP-BOOK

A Semi-Monthly Miscellany and Review of Belles-Lettres. Price, 10 cents a copy; $2.00 a year.

"The *Chap-Book* is indispensable. In its new form, as a literary review, it fills an important place in our magazine literature."—*Rochester Post-Express.*

"The new *Chap-Book* is an imposing and inspiring production to take in the hands, and it is opened with an anticipatory zest that is rewarded simply by a reading of the contents."—*Providence News.*

"The notes are vivacious and vigorous. The literary quality is what one has a right to expect from a literary journal, and we heartily welcome the new *Chap-Book* to our table."—*The Watchman.*

"In its enlarged form the magazine has taken on a somewhat more serious aspect than it carried in its first estate, but it has lost none of its crispness and interest."—*Brooklyn Eagle.*

"As we glance through the *Chap-Book* we are newly charmed with the excellence of its book reviews. Of course it has other features of interest —notably the introductory "notes" that give in a genteel way the freshest gossip of the aristocracy of letters—but for our part we turn at once to the book reviews, for we know that there we can be sure of being at once instructed and entertained. Whoever they are that produce this copy—and being anonymous, one has no clue—they deserve rich recompense of cakes and wine, and, betimes, a lift in salary, for they do know how to review." —*Scranton Tribune.*

THE HOUSE BEAUTIFUL

A Monthly Magazine devoted to Houses and Homes. Articles on Rugs, Furniture, Pottery, Silverware, and Bookbindings; Prints, Engravings, and Etchings; Interior and Exterior Decoration, etc. Abundantly illustrated. t is a magazine of general interest, and appreciative rather than technical n character. 10 cents a copy; $1.00 a year. Sample copies sent for five wo-cent stamps.

"*The House Beautiful,* for its sincerity of purpose and dignified fulilment of its aim, so far, should be highly commended, The third number ontains some exquisite illustrations.   *   *   Some good reviews and otes follow the articles, and a really useful magazine, in a fair way to become well established, is thus kept on its course."—*Chicago Times-Herald.*

"Throughout, this magazine is governed by good taste to a degree which s almost unique."—*Indianapolis News.*

"There is room for a magazine like *The House Beautiful,* and the hird number of that excellent monthly indicates that the void is in a fair ay to be filled. In addition to a good assortment of articles on practical uestions of household art and artisanship, there is a valuable paper by W· rving Way on ' Women and Bookbinding '."—*Chicago Tribune.*

"*The House Beautiful* is the title of the new monthly which deals rincipally with art as applied to industry and the household.   *   *   It ems to be a magazine which will have a permanent use and interest."— *Vorcester Spy.*

For sale by all Booksellers and Newsdealers, or will be sent, postpaid, by the publishers, on receipt of price.

HERBERT S. STONE & COMPANY

axton Bldg, Chicago   Constable Bldg., New York

www.ingramcontent.com/pod-product-compliance
Lightning Source LLC
Chambersburg PA
CBHW030318240426
43673CB00040B/1201